THE GOSPEL OF JOHN, THE GOSPEL OF RELATIONSHIP

The Gospel of John, The Gospel of Relationship

Jean Vanier

Franciscan
MEDIA
Cincinnati, Ohio

Scripture quotations are from the author's own translation.

Cover and book design by Mark Sullivan
Cover image © Fotolia | Lijuan Guo

LIBRARY OF CONGRESS CATALOGING-IN-PUBLICATION DATA
Vanier, Jean, 1928-
The Gospel of John, the gospel of relationship / Jean Vanier.
pages cm
ISBN 978-1-61636-890-6 (paperback)
1. Bible. John—Commentaries. 2. Love—Religious aspects—
Christianity. 3. Interpersonal relations—Religious aspects—
Christianity. I. Title.
BS2615.53.V365 2015
226.5'06—dc23
                                          2015003941

ISBN 978-1-61636-890-6

Published by Franciscan Media
28 W. Liberty St.
Cincinnati, OH 45202
www.FranciscanMedia.org

Printed in the United States of America.
Printed on acid-free paper.
15 16 17 18 19   5 4 3 2 1

Contents

This book has its origins in a series of videos on the Gospel of John, which were filmed in the Holy Land in 2010. Because it cannot say all that is contained in this beautiful Gospel, I chose passages that I felt were important to reveal what is particular to John. I made a few corrections to this written transcript of the videos in order to clarify the text. This book is a foretaste of the Gospel and should be completed by other works on the Gospel of John, including Drawn into the Mystery of Jesus through the Gospel of John, which I wrote in 2004.

My hope is that all that I have received from John may be shared with many others. John has formed my heart, my prayer, my life, my spirituality, and my theology. I am grateful to him. May each of us become, as he was, a beloved friend of Jesus.

I feel privileged and a little humbled to write about the Gospel of John, because it is such an extraordinary Gospel, one that draws us into the mystery of God—into the heart of God himself. It reveals to us the Father and reveals to us the vulnerability and love of Jesus. This Gospel is very different from the other three Gospels—those of Matthew, Mark, and Luke. It is clear that while John knew of these other Gospels, he reveals events that they do not.

Who Is the Author?

The Gospel of John was written around A.D. 90–95 by someone who calls himself "the Beloved Disciple." Did this disciple think Jesus loved him more than he loved the others? No. Rather, this name reveals to us this disciple's deepest identity, which is also the deepest identity of each one of us. Our identity is not, as people often think, our role or what we do. Our deepest need is to be loved, and our deepest identity is to be the beloved of Jesus.

The author of this Gospel is most likely John, the brother of James; both were sons of Zebedee. Through Ireneaus and Clement of Alexandria in the early Church, we understand that he was the disciple who rested on the heart of Jesus, and who received Mary at the foot of the cross as his mother. In the early third century, Origen said that to understand this Gospel one must first have rested on the heart of Jesus and taken Mary as one's mother.

The author of this Gospel seeks historical accuracy about dates, time, places, and Jewish feast days. He is deeply Jewish, infused by the vision and the spirituality of the Torah, the prophets, and the books of wisdom. John, deeply rooted in Judaism, is a privileged witness to Jesus—to his life, his vision, and his person.

Why Was This Gospel Written?

Why did John write this book? He explains clearly, at the end of chapter 20, that it was written "so that you may believe that Jesus is the Messiah and the Son of God, and that in believing you will have life in his name." It was written that we will have life! This is the Gospel of life, written so that we might become fully living! What is this life? For Aristotle, life is everything that moves and has movement from within. But what does this life move toward?

For John, life is relationship, life is communion—especially the life and communion in God, with God, and with each other. The Gospel of John is the Gospel of relationship, and we will see it tells of a growing relationship with Jesus. It has a beginning. There is a meeting, which grows into a friendship. In friendship we abide or dwell one in another. There is growth, and then there is a fecundity, the desire to give life. In this Gospel of relationship, we learn to grow in love. It is a spiritual journey; it is growth into a deeper communion with Jesus, a friendship with Jesus and through him with his Father.

The big question for us human beings is: Who is God, and who is Jesus? Growth comes through the gradual discovery of the vulnerability of Jesus, the Word who became flesh. It will be an emerging understanding that in his fragility, he is giving us life. At the same time, through this Gospel, we will better understand who *we* are, with our fragility, our vulnerability, our fears, and our prejudices. We will come to understand our own need to be transformed by Jesus, who came to reveal the Father to each of us.

The Gospel of Transformation

This is not only the Gospel of relationship but also of transformation. All relationships start through the body. The first relationship is that between a mother and her little baby, to whom she tenderly gives life. The mother says to the child through gestures and words: "You are precious to me." There can also be moments of wounding, when the child does not meet the expectations of the mother, or the mother does not respond to the needs of the child. Thus there are moments of brokenness in their communion. A healthy relationship is not always simple. It is not possessive or controlling, nor is it being absent. Relationship implies a purification. The mother is called to respect the child profoundly, saying, "You are different, and you are uniquely precious to me." However, for the mother to separate from the child, and to encourage the child to grow in freedom, can be painful and difficult. She must be purified so that her child can remain "other," become fully himself or herself, and not be suffocated by the relationship. Our humanity grows and develops in relationships through which we are transformed and grow in freedom.

All this happens in and through the body. John is very careful to make clear that Jesus is fully human: There were moments when Jesus was tired or anguished. John lived in an era when both within and outside the community of believers there were those who denied that Jesus was really human. Therefore, the whole message of John attempts to show that Jesus did have a physical body, and that presence and communion are transmitted through the body. The Word became flesh. We will discover through this Gospel that human beings need to be gradually transformed, body and soul, to enter into a fullness of love.

This Gospel Incorporates All That John Received from Mary

In this Gospel, we discover something special. The last words of Jesus on the cross are: "Woman, here is your son"; then he looks at John and says, "Here is your mother." It is said that "from that moment, he [John] took Mary as his own," as his treasure. Thereafter John lived with Mary.

As the mother of Jesus, Mary naturally had an intimate physical relationship with him. Jesus had lived nine months in her womb, had suckled at her breast, and was nourished by her milk. Mary thus had a knowledge and experience of Jesus that nobody else did. For about thirty years, she and Jesus lived together with Joseph.

Obviously, the story told by John, about who Jesus is and who God is, will be uniquely influenced by John's relationship with Mary. Jesus said to John, "Here is your mother." He did not say, "Welcome *my* mother." He said, "Here is *your* mother." Thus, we can assume that John carefully chose events to tell us about Jesus in the light of the gentle understanding John received concerning Jesus through his own special relationship with Mary.

CHAPTER ONE

The Vulnerability of the Logos Who Becomes Flesh
(JOHN 1:1–18)

The Prologue: An Extraordinary Poetic Vision

The Gospel of John starts with a marvelous prologue: "In the beginning, before all things were, the Logos was. The Logos was with God, present to God, turned toward God; and the Logos was God. In the beginning the Logos was with God."

I would like to say something about the meaning of *logos*. It is often translated as "word." But *logos* is broader in meaning: It is the vision or the plan of God—the inspiration behind the spoken word. The "word" and the "thought" of God are the same. In fact, I would dare to call *logos* "wisdom."

Thus we have: "In the beginning there was the mind of God, the wisdom of God, and the wisdom was with God." Here there is the little Greek word *pros*: the Word is in relationship with God; we translate it "near to God" or "toward God," but I sometimes like to say, "the Word was in communion with God."

It is interesting that Goethe, for example, says, "In the beginning was action." In the Gospel of John it is said, "In the beginning, before all things were, there was unity and communion." This unity precedes creation. From this primary unity comes the unity of all creation. This is an extraordinary vision!

"All things were made through him, and without him nothing was made that was made. In him was life, and life was the light of every person." The beauty of creation is the unity of all, a marvelous unity of love! Moreover, at the heart of this mystery is the unity of man and woman.

We will discover in this extraordinary chapter that there is also darkness, brokenness, and shadows. The shadows came, but they never overcame the Light, nor stopped the Light from shining through the darkness. The history of humanity is a marvelous story of great prophets. They showed the way toward God, the way of truth, the way that people may choose to find their fulfillment, but people did not accept the Light they preached.

The prologue ends: "The Word became flesh." The Word that is in communion with God, this Word that is at the heart of all things and at the source of creation, became flesh. John does not write that the Word became a human being, but that the Word became *flesh*, and flesh is a fragile reality. Flesh and blood are fragile, vulnerable, and dependent. The Word became flesh!

This is the great mystery that is revealed through the Gospel of John. Before, heaven and earth, the infinite and the finite, had been divided. Now, there is unity. The infinity of the Word enters into the finitude of matter: They become one in a body, in flesh. The Word of God, who is God, who is one with God, becomes one of us: a fragile, vulnerable human being.

This Logos became a little child, hidden in the womb of a woman. The infinite became little. In a suffering and broken creation, the Word became flesh. He is the presence of God on earth. He has appeared as something new. In the silence of the Annunciation, the woman has borne fruit; she has given new life through the power of the Holy Spirit. "The Word became flesh," and he pitched his tent among us; he came as a pilgrim among us all. He came to guide us toward God, to help us know a God of love, of tenderness, and of forgiveness. He came to reveal to us who God is, because previously the history of humanity had been a history of many people living in fear of God.

"The Word became flesh." In one translation of the prologue, it is written: "The only Son is turned toward the heart of the Father, and reveals him to us." There is another translation that seems closer to the truth: "The Word, the only Son, came to guide us into the heart of the Father, into oneness with the Father." This is the mystery, and John expresses it clearly: The law was given by Moses. Jesus came to bring us grace, truth, and love—freely given in tenderness.

It is extraordinary for me to write of the Gospel of John while I am in Bethlehem, because it is here that the Word made flesh was born. It is important for us to remember that the initiative comes from God. Jesus says, "It is I who have chosen you." Indeed, all of the Gospel of John reveals the initiatives of God. "God so loved the world that he sent his only Son, so that, in believing in him, we might have eternal life, and we might be saved."

Yes, this Gospel begins: "The Word became flesh" (John 3:16).

The Bond with L'Arche

I love the Gospel of John, and it has clarified my understanding of L'Arche and Faith and Light.[1] I believe that this

Gospel is special for L'Arche. Why? John speaks in a unique way about love. The Gospel of John, as I have said, is the Gospel of relationship, and L'Arche and Faith and Light are schools of relationship.

I have had the privilege of living in L'Arche for more than fifty years now, with people who have often been rejected because of their disabilities. What do people with a disability want? The most profound desire of the oppressed, and of each of us in our poverty, is for a true relationship. This is the whole meaning of L'Arche. It is not a matter of doing good deeds for people with a disability or people who are oppressed and humiliated. It is not a matter of *giving* things to them. True relationship implies helping others to discover who they truly are, respected and loved in their deepest person and called to rise up as they are to find their place in the world or in the Church.

The aim of this Gospel is to help every one of us to discover that we are all beautiful children of God. The prologue says, "All those who believed in him have become children of God." L'Arche is a place where each one of us with and without visible disabilities can grow in love and develop together, so that we can reclaim the extraordinary dignity of our common humanity, as well as our call to become beloved children of God and to work together for the unity of the human family and of creation.

CHAPTER TWO

John the Baptist: Witness for Jesus
(JOHN 1:19–50)

"There was a man, and his name was John. He was sent by God to be a witness, to testify to the Light, so that all might believe through him. He was not the Light." The Word was the true Light. John the Baptist says of Jesus: "After me comes One who was before me." John focuses his followers upon Jesus.

Everyone comes to John, and he baptizes them with water. He announces the path toward God, and he says that someone else will come after him. He tells the people to follow the ways of God: "If you have two coats, give one to the poor."

John says, "I am not the Messiah." So then, who *is* John? "I am the voice of one crying out in the wilderness, 'Make, straight the way of the Lord,' as the prophet Isaiah said." John says of Jesus: "Behold, the Lamb of God!"

Why Does Jesus Need a Witness?
Why was it necessary to have a preparation for the coming of Jesus and to have someone who would witness to him? Jesus's coming was prepared for in two ways. First, there were Mary and Joseph. Jesus had to be welcomed by Mary, welcomed into the flesh of a woman, his mother. He had to be welcomed by Joseph. He lived simply for thirty years with his parents

in Nazareth. It was important that the Word made flesh would live out the message of the Beatitudes before he would announce it.

Second, there was the preparation for the coming of Jesus through the powerful message of John the Baptist, a prophet. John wore a camel-hair coat and he ate just a little bit of wild honey. He cried out like a prophet, and he baptized people in the river. Many people were drawn to him.

Unlike John, Jesus himself did not appear to be in any way remarkable. In his humility, he looked more or less like everyone else. He ate with prostitutes and sinners. It was necessary that there would be a prophet to point toward Jesus and say, "It is he, follow him."

The mission of John the Baptist was to witness, to announce, and to incite a movement toward Jesus to prepare people to welcome Jesus. John was a humble witness. Sometimes the danger with witnesses is that they draw attention to themselves. Not so with John, who clearly says, "It is *he!*" A little later, John says, "The bride is the one who is *with* the bridegroom. The friend of the bridegroom rejoices simply to hear the bridegroom's voice. This is my joy, that he grows and that I diminish." The story of John the Baptist is that he must disappear and Jesus must have more prominence (see John 3:29–30).

John baptized with water, and even Jesus himself came to be baptized. When John had baptized Jesus, a dove descended and rested upon Jesus. At that moment, John realized in a unique way that here was the one who was to come, the chosen one of God. Though John baptized in the waters of purification, Jesus would baptize in the Spirit.

Here Is the Lamb of God

At one moment John sees Jesus from afar, walking humbly without drawing attention to himself, and he cries out, "Pay close attention! Behold, here is the Lamb of God, who takes away the sin of the world!"

What an extraordinary pronouncement! A lamb is not something strong—on the contrary, a lamb is small, weak, and at the mercy of others. Yet, Jesus is called the *lamb*. For the Jewish people, the symbolism of the lamb was familiar and profound. John's words take us back to the third chapter of Exodus and beyond. There we read that God called Moses, saying, "I have seen the misery of my people," and God sent Moses to liberate them. However, the Pharaoh did not cooperate, so God sent several tribulations. In preparation for the final tribulation, God warned the Jews to mark their doorways with the blood of a lamb, so that when God sent the angel of death to kill the firstborn sons of the Egyptians, the angel would pass over the houses marked with the blood of the lamb. This is the Passover. This is Easter. This is the great moment of liberation.

We must remember this story, because through this ancient vision we are told that it is blood of the lamb that will liberate the Jewish people. Moses heard the call of God, "Set my people free!" He led the Jews away from their lives of slavery and across the Red Sea to freedom. Easter is the time of remembrance of this extraordinary moment in Jewish history, a celebration of liberation.

Jesus is the true Lamb who came to liberate us—but from what? He came to liberate us from our sins. What are our sins? Our sins are refusing the love of God and of people. We isolate ourselves with elaborate systems of defense around our hearts. These protective walls keep us away from those who are different. Fear and hate are born, and borders are erected between individuals and entire groups of people. Jesus came to liberate each of us from this entrapment of our hearts so that we may love others as he loves them.

At the time of John the Baptist, there were many young people searching. There were also the zealots, who hated the Romans. Flavius Josephus, a Jew who in A.D. 100 wrote the history of the Jewish people, mentions something that was not written in John's Gospel. He describes something horrible: an uprising that started in Galilee, the date of which we are uncertain. Different than the Judeans, the Galileans were a strong people who often struggled for liberation through violence. The Romans called them terrorists. During this particular revolution, which was unsettling to the Romans, the emperor sent Varius from Damascus to crush the rebellion. Flavius Josephus writes that the Romans then crucified two thousand Galileans. Yes, they crucified *two thousand* Galileans! We can imagine the hate and the anger in the Galileans: "They crucified my son, my uncle, my father!" The Jews hated the Romans and were seeking liberation from them. They were waiting for the Messiah who would throw out the Romans and allow the Jewish people to reclaim their dignity.

Jesus, however, is something else! The Lamb of God did not come liberate the Jewish people from the Romans but to liberate each one of us from our hate, from our fear of difference, and from our desire for power. The lamb is also spoken of in Isaiah 53, which describes the vision of the suffering and sorrowing servant, who prefigures Jesus crucified. There, too, we discover how the Lamb will liberate us:

> He was afflicted, without any beauty or comeliness, despised and rejected, and we believed him to be punished by God, but through his wounds we are healed.... He was like a lamb led to slaughter. (Isaiah 53:2, 7)

The Lamb of God, who takes away the sin of the world, takes away our refusal of God and all that separates our hearts from God. What is it that separates our hearts from God? It is our refusal to welcome others who are different, the poor, and those in need. Jesus came to liberate us—you and me—from our fear and violence and hatred, to teach us to love with wisdom.

The First Disciples of Jesus

The day after John points out Jesus as the Lamb of God, John is there again, with at least two of his disciples. We will learn that one of these was Andrew, but the other is not named. We suspect that the other is John the Evangelist, a son of Zebedee and the brother of James. John the Baptist sees Jesus and says again, "Look closely! Behold, the Lamb of God." These two disciples leave John the Baptist and begin to follow Jesus. Humbly, John lets them go. Jesus turns toward them and asks them a question. These are the first words of Jesus in the Gospel of John, so they are significant. Jesus looks at them and asks, "What are you searching for?" The disciples are perhaps a little lost, and it is touching that Jesus asks them, "What do you want?" Perhaps Jesus asks each of us that same question today, "What are you looking for? What are you searching for, in coming today to hear the Gospel of John?"

Not expecting such a question, they are uncertain and respond, "Teacher, where do you dwell?" I suppose that they just want to spend time with Jesus. John had proclaimed Jesus as the Lamb of God who would take away the sin of the world; he is someone important in the ways of God. They want to spend time with him. Jesus answers, "Come and see." This Gospel of John is going to lead us to where Jesus dwells. We are invited, like the disciples, to come and see in this Gospel.

There is a touching detail here in the text, when John the Evangelist says, "It was four o'clock in the afternoon." I have an image, as I read that, of the old John years later as he is writing the Gospel, saying to himself, "I remember the first time I met Jesus ..." Perhaps each of us should ask ourselves this question: When was the very first time I met Jesus, and that I felt my heart open to the universal and the infinite?

Here we have the first two companions of Jesus. Afterward, Andrew hurries off to find his brother, Peter, and says to him, "We have found the Messiah," and he brings Peter to Jesus. After that, they meet Philip, and Jesus looks at him and says, "Follow me." Philip is moved by Jesus and hurries off to find his friend Nathaniel, saying to him, "We have found the Messiah!"

So, we have this first small group of men eagerly following Jesus, without really knowing where they are going. The cry of John the Baptist: "Here is the Lamb of God!" reso-nates in their hearts. Jesus is leading them to discover a new freedom—not the *political* liberation of the Jewish people, but an inner freedom, the liberation of their hearts, so that they can live an intimate encounter with God, whom they will discover as their Father. They will also discover that it is in this quiet way that Jesus came to bring peace to the world.

Following Jesus: Witnesses to a New Love

The five men who were drawn to Jesus will become witnesses to the love of Jesus, witnesses to who God is, and witnesses to the new love that can change the world.

However, it is not just those five men who were called to be witnesses to this love; it is all of us. It is you and I. The world does not need only important people as witnesses, although of course we need people like Nelson Mandela, John Paul II, Martin Luther King, Jr., Gandhi, Mother Teresa, and others to be witnesses to the truth of love. Each of us, you and I, are also called to be witnesses through the love we show one another. As Jesus said, "They will know you are my disciples by the love you have for one another" (John 13:35). Living simply together, with love and tenderness, and celebrating the joy of being together: these are the signs of our love for one another.

There have also been less prominent witnesses, such as Rosa Parks, a black American seamstress in Atlanta in the sixties, who refused to give up her seat on the bus to a white person, as the civil regulations required. In doing so, she started a boycott of the segregated buses, a movement of solidarity that financially crippled the transit system and that eventually culminated in Martin Luther King's speech, "I Have a Dream."

In our time, this dream was realized with the presidency of Barack Obama. Yet, it was this humble woman who set that dream in motion.

Sophie Scholl, a young German girl of twenty-two, also started something extraordinary. In 1943, she refused to follow Gestapo orders. She had heard that the SS had been killing Jews in Poland. She said, "No!" and began to distribute antiwar tracts explaining how to resist a dictator through nonviolence. She was asked during her trial, "Why were you doing this?" She replied, "Many people think as I do, and it is important that someone started to say it in public!" She and her brother Hans, who helped her, were both executed at the guillotine.

There have been others as well, not well-known figures, but people like you and me. It is up to each of us to be liberated from the tyranny of normality and injustice. Then each of us may be liberated to love.

This message of Jesus is so simple. He reveals a vision of love, where the rejected and the weak have the central place. It is they who call us to act! Their cry for love and justice awakens a new force within us. Perhaps today, if we work together with the rejected and the weak, we can all rise up to create a new world together. So it is they, the weak and the rejected, who are our prophets. It is they who are a presence of God among us.

CHAPTER THREE

The Wedding at Cana:
The Key to Understanding This Gospel
(JOHN 2:1–12)

As we've seen, John the Baptist has just named Jesus "the Lamb." Two of his disciples, Andrew and probably John the Evangelist, start to follow the Lamb. They stay with Jesus. Afterward, Andrew seeks out Simon, whom Jesus will call the Rock, Peter, announcing: "We have found the Messiah!" Then they meet Philip, and Jesus says to Philip, "Follow me!" Philip then hurries to find Nathaniel, saying "We have found the Messiah!" This is how the little group of five around Jesus begins— the group that will become the origin of the Church.

Where is Jesus leading them? One could imagine that he will lead them into the desert, somewhere to meditate on the Torah and the Prophets, or to pray together. But, in fact, he takes them to a wonderful celebration, a marriage feast!

Jesus goes to the wedding to celebrate; he is wonderfully human. He goes there to be with the members of his family and friends, all the people he knew from Nazareth and the surrounding area.

It is important to understand that at that time in Israel wedding feasts were grandiose and lasted a week. There was a lot of drinking, so much so that the linguistic root of the Aramaic words for *wedding* and *drink* are the same! So, this small group was going with Jesus simply to meet with friends and family to celebrate, to sing, and certainly to drink! But this wedding feast at Cana also symbolizes and reveals another wedding feast.

Our Final Destiny: The Wedding Feast of Love

Why did Jesus the Lamb take his disciples to this wedding? Perhaps he was revealing the mystery of the covenant destined for all of us. Jesus invites us to enter into an intimate relationship with him, into a friendship or communion with him, which is an alliance or a covenant. And this covenant is also communion with his Father. It is a celebration of love as in a wedding feast.

In the nineteenth and twenty-first chapters of the book of Revelation, heaven is described as the wedding feast of the Lamb:

> Let us be filled with joy and gladness. It is the wedding feast of the Lamb, and the bride has made herself beautiful; she is ready for her husband!" (Revelation 19:7–10)

That is life in heaven: It is a wonderful place of celebration, of wedding festivities, and of love—a place where there will be no more suffering or death, for the former things have passed way (see Revelation 21: 4).

The vision of Jesus, even on earth, is to invite us to enter into a loving relationship with him, so we may live in him and he in us. We can read this, for example, in the book of Hosea, where God is calling his people into a relationship of love:

> I will seduce her [the unfaithful woman]. I will lead
> her into the desert and I will speak to her heart. I
> will engage her to me forever. I will engage her to me
> through justice and righteousness, through love and
> tenderness. I will engage her to me in faithfulness,
> and thus you will know the Lord. (Hosea 2:14)

In Isaiah 62, it is even more extraordinary! We read that the
bride will be the delight of God. God, the spouse, will wed
his beloved ones, and they will be his joy. We can see that this
mystery is gradually being unveiled through the symbol of the
wedding feast of Cana.

Human Marriage

Human marriage is something beautiful: A man and a woman
are called to live as one body, in the unity of a loving and
faithful relationship. This relationship is expressed with their
whole beings, their hearts and their bodies. They accept each
other completely, in humility and tenderness. It is a vision
of sexuality for a faithful relationship, for a life of oneness
that will be fruitful. Marriage symbolically represents our
encounter with God through Jesus, through the body of Jesus.
It is through the Eucharist that Jesus gives us his Body to eat
and his Blood to drink, so that we can dwell in him and he in
us. Jesus came to lead us into oneness with him and to help
us live a life of oneness with others. The whole mystery and
mission of Jesus is to dissolve the barriers that prevent us from
meeting with and loving each other.

Let us come back to the wedding feast at Cana. Jesus has
come to celebrate, but there is some drama. Mary, who is

behind the scenes, perhaps helping, notices that there is no more wine.

"They Have No More Wine"

This, of course, is enormously humiliating to the hosts. Mary is very sensitive to the suffering of the poor. Here are two families, both probably quite poor, about to be humiliated because there is no more wine. So Mary goes to find Jesus and tells him, "They have no more wine." Jesus replies, "Woman, what is there between you and me? My time has not yet come."

This reply of Jesus was enigmatic. Behind this statement of Jesus lies something profound. This wedding feast was the final moment of Jesus's hidden life with Mary in Nazareth. Now it was time for him to attend to the affairs of his Father. His mission was to announce to the world the message of love, forgiveness, and the value of each person. However, he was well aware that this message of love would provoke opposition, and that people would not want to hear it, because they wanted to hold on to whatever power they possessed. He knew that this path would lead to his rejection, to conflict, and finally "when his time has come" to condemnation on the cross. So, in a way, Jesus was saying to Mary, "I'll meet you at the cross," where he would give life to all of us.

Mary has so much confidence in her beloved son that she goes to the servants and tells them, "Do whatever he says!" They accept this instruction, just as Mary had said yes to God's messenger.

Jesus tells the servants to fill six large jars to the top with water. The servants, a bit surprised, hurry back and forth from the well to fill the jars. It must have taken many buckets, and they were probably tired. For miracles to take place, humble servants are needed!

The servants then bring the water changed into wine to the master of ceremonies, who tastes it and is astonished! He says to the bridal couple: "You have saved the best wine until now? Usually the best wine is served at the beginning, and then once the guests are a little drunk, the cheaper wine is served."

This miracle is important. It revealed the power of Jesus, and the disciples believed in him. A touching note: Each of those huge jars contained twenty or thirty gallons—so, Jesus transformed 120 or perhaps even 180 gallons of water into a wonderful wine even though people were already a little tipsy. Someone like me might have said, "Oh, that's too much wine! Change only a hundred gallons!" With Jesus, there is always an abundance of gifts and of love.

The Deeper Meaning of the Wedding Feast

The most profound meaning of the story of Cana is the sign of the transformation of water into wine. We are each called to love—to love now on earth and to reach the banquet of love in heaven. We need to change; we need to be transformed. In our human hearts, there are many fears—fear of others, fear even of God—so there needs to be a gradual transformation to a heart of love. We will discover that the Gospel of John is the Gospel of transformation. It is the Gospel of the deepening of faith and of love. Transformation implies that we become aware of our inabilities, vulnerabilities, and darkness—all those areas within us that need to be transformed.

This miracle at Cana also has special meaning for us at L'Arche. When we read Matthew 22, we are told that the kingdom of heaven is like a wedding feast—yes, a wedding feast! In this passage, Jesus tells the story of a king who had prepared a wonderful banquet for the wedding of his son. He sent invitations to all the dignitaries and important people of his kingdom. They all replied, "I don't have time, I am too busy, I have many things to do. I have just bought some land; I have to build on it. I have just bought some cattle; I must care for them. I have to get my daughter married; sorry, I am too busy." This story is a prophecy: It reveals that many people are too busy with social events to receive the message of love of Jesus. They are busy with the desire for power and possessions. "I do not have time because of my social class, and I must show my importance. I am sorry but I cannot attend." Of course, the heart of the king was wounded. Like Jesus, he had invited them to a banquet of love, and nobody wanted to come! So, what happened? The king told the servants, "Go out into the streets and the villages and bring in to the feast the poor, the lame, and the blind."

He told them to bring in people with disabilities, people on the margins of society who are often rejected and have too *much* time on their hands. Their worry is not about power, possessions, or fame. The main thing the disabled and disenfranchised want is a relationship of friendship and of love. So, these people rushed to partake in the banquet of love.

We Are All Made for Love

We are all made for love and to grow in love. Many people with disabilities and especially those with a severe disability may not be able to marry. However, they, too, are made for love and for the discovery that they are beautiful and that they are precious in their bodies. They, too, are called to an encounter with God, the God of peace. We are all invited to the wedding feast.

I would like to tell a touching story that took place in our L'Arche community in Kerala, India. Chris Sadler welcomed Ramesh into the community there. Ramesh was a man with an intellectual disability, and he was also epileptic. He had spent many long years in a psychiatric hospital (which I have visited myself, and which was quite horrible) with locked cells. About three years ago, Ramesh, by then living in our community, went to spend the weekend with his brother. At the end of the weekend, he visited the neighbors there and told them, "Tomorrow is my marriage day, the day of my wedding." Everyone smiled a little, as is often the case when someone with an intellectual disability says something people do not really understand. He then got on the bus, arrived back at the community, and went into the workshop where everyone was working. He told them, too, "Tomorrow will be my wedding day." Later that night, he went to sleep, had a heart attack, and died.

How can we interpret his words about his wedding day? For many people with disabilities, the greatest joy in life is the wedding celebration, the marriage. They wish to celebrate in this way themselves as a sign that they are like everyone else. Perhaps Ramesh was sensing something deep within himself, that he would soon experience an enormous joy! In his own way, then, Ramesh interpreted this sense by announcing, "Tomorrow will be my wedding day." We are all made to love and to share in the wedding feast.

At L'Arche, we have discovered something else: Deep within, we are all made for joyful celebrations! For human beings, the meal is very important as a place of celebration. We are made to celebrate; we are made to be men and women of joy and unity! "Love one another": that is our calling. One of the founding texts of L'Arche is the lesson told in Luke 14 in which Jesus says:

> When you give a meal, don't invite the members of your family, your friends, or your rich neighbors, who can repay you by inviting you back. Rather, when you give a banquet, invite the poor, the lame, the maimed, and the blind, and *you will be blessed*.

This is a blessing, a beatitude! In the truest sense, to eat at a table with the poor and those who are rejected and marginalized is to become their friend. In the biblical meaning, eating together means entering into an alliance and friendship. So we learn: "Become a friend of the poor, and you will be blessed." More deeply, it is also a beatitude to work for unity, to break down the walls that separate people from those who are rejected.

Therefore, that the Lamb takes his disciples to the wedding feast reveals much. The wedding feast is a sign of heaven; it is love and it is relationship. To live this relationship, the water of our humanity must gradually be transformed by the Holy Spirit into the wine of love. This wine of love is also the wine transformed into the Blood of Jesus. We are all made for love. Those who love truly love others as they are, for themselves, and freely. The Lamb who loves us seeks to be united to us so that we can become fully ourselves. Jesus does not seek to possess or control us, but he wants to help us completely fulfill our mission and vocation. The wedding feast at Cana speaks to us of the wedding feast of the Lamb in heaven. It speaks to all people; we are all called to work toward and to celebrate unity and peace.

CHAPTER FOUR

The New Temple: The Body of Jesus
(JOHN 2:13–25)

Where does God live? Where can we find God, or have an experience of God? Is God interested in the pain and brokenness of our world? These are central questions for us today.

Where is God?—this was the cry of people in concentration camps; it is the cry of people who are being bombed or tortured or who are in excruciating pain. This is the question we will look at now.

When the Hebrew people had passed from slavery to freedom and had been led through the Red Sea, there burst forth from Moses a song of thanksgiving for the glory of God. For forty years, they had wandered through the desert. God, through Moses, had asked the people to build a "tent of meeting," and within that tent there was a sanctuary with the ark of the covenant. This sanctuary was shrouded with a cloud, symbolizing the presence and the glory of God. For forty years, the people of God were guided during the day by this cloud, and at night by a column of fire.

Many years after this, Solomon, the son of King David, built a more permanent and very large Temple for God, a dwelling place or home for God. He constructed something grand. When the priests brought the ark of the covenant into the sanctuary of this Temple, the cloud, the presence of God, enfolded the sanctuary.

Years later, another temple was built, this time by Herod, after Solomon's had been destroyed. Again what was built was grand. The temple for the Jewish people was the place of their identity. It was a constant reminder for them that their God had uniquely chosen the Jewish people. They were his people. To honor their God, Jewish people from afar went on pilgrimages to Jerusalem. Jesus himself went on pilgrimage to the Temple of Jerusalem to celebrate the Passover, as well as for the Feast of the Dedication of the Temple and the Feast of Tents. The spirit of the people beginning these pilgrimages is captured in the words of Psalm 122: "I was glad when they said to me: Let us go to the house of the Lord."

Jesus Reveals to Us That His Body Is the New Temple of God

In the second chapter of John's Gospel, we find Jesus in Jerusalem. As a Jew, he of course goes to the Temple of God, the house of prayer. But what does he find there? In the Temple he finds the stalls of merchants and money changers. The Temple has become a marketplace, where animals are available to be bought for sacrifices. The money changers are changing Greek and Roman coins into special Temple money, and the rates of exchange they offer are excessive and oppressive. As Jesus perceives that the sacredness of the house of God has been defiled and made unholy, anger and tears overcome him. The Temple has become a place of exploitation, even more so because the poor cannot afford the exorbitant prices being asked for the animals. So Jesus takes a whip, drives out all the animals, and turns the money tables upside down, scattering the money onto the floor. Jesus is left with tears of anger in his eyes at this desecration of the house of God. Obviously, the Temple authorities come running, demanding, "What authority do you have? What signs have you accomplished that give you the right to act in this way?" Jesus responds surprisingly, "Destroy this sanctuary, and in three days I will raise it up." The priests of the Temple sneer: "It took forty-six years to build this Temple, and you will rebuild it in three days?" They laugh at him and mock him.

There is an important detail here. We have now been clearly shown by John the year in which all this took place. We know that the building of the Temple was started about nineteen or twenty years before the birth of Jesus. Thus, forty-six years later puts the date about the year A.D. 27 or 28. This is an example of the small, but important, details that John provides us in his Gospel.

"Destroy this sanctuary, and in three days I will raise it up." John explains: "Jesus was speaking of the sanctuary of his body." So, it is the body of Jesus that is the new Temple, the Temple of God, the presence of God. The Jewish people of that time regarded a permanent, huge, and beautiful Temple as the place where God lives. Jesus, however, is a person with a body, beautiful but fragile like all human bodies and both delicate and sensitive. This is the new Temple of God, not made of beautiful stones; it is a person of flesh and blood with whom we can be in relationship. Jesus invites us to pray to an intimate God who is near us, with us, and in us, one whose heart can be wounded, a God such as the prophets knew—not a God who would allow the exploitation of the poor. Even when this body is bleeding, wounded, and broken on the cross, it is still the home of God, the place where God dwells on earth.

The word *dwell* in the Gospel of John is an important word, and it is found throughout the text. Jesus calls us to dwell in his love. He also says, "If someone loves me and keeps my word, my Father will love him, and we will come and make our dwelling place in him" (John 14:23).

Our Bodies Are the Temple of God

Jesus brings us a message that is startling and new: He is the dwelling place of God, the presence of God, but each of us is called to be the dwelling place of God. St. Paul, in his Letter to the Corinthians, says, "Do you not know that you are the temple of God and that God's Spirit dwells in you? God's temple is holy, and you are that temple." These are strong words! Jesus says, "I dwell in you and you in me" (1 Corinthians 3:16). This is radically new. We are, each one of us, the dwelling place of God, and the Church is the dwelling place of God as well. It is important to help each other to become aware of this.

Some years ago, we welcomed in our L'Arche community a young man named Eric who had a severe disability. He was blind and deaf and could not walk. He, too, is loved by God; he, too, is the dwelling place of God. Those who are in a state of great impairment, those who are pulled into the terrors of addiction, alcoholism, or drugs, are called to be the dwelling place of God, just as all of us are. Often people do not understand that the whole mystery of human beings is that we are made to be and become the presence of God. God dwells even in the most wounded and fragile people.

Etty Hillesum, a young Jewish Dutch woman killed in Auschwitz, said something very beautiful when she was in the concentration camp at Westerbork: "You cannot help us, God, but we must help you and defend your dwelling place inside of us, to the very last."[2]

What does it mean to defend God's dwelling place inside of us? In this chapter, Jesus is revealing a rivalry between Mammon—money—and God. It is clear that we need money to live and to share. The danger is that we want to have more and more things, more and more money. We can even become obsessed with this desire, and it can overcome and destroy us. God wants to liberate us, to reveal that our bodies are beautiful. They are not to be defiled or made unholy by obsession with money. God is asking us to discover that our bodies are more than merely physical—they are the place where God dwells. We are all called to be the temple of God.

Conflict between the Temple and Mercy

In the time of Solomon, the Temple was the sacred place for the Jewish people. When the priest brought the ark of the covenant into the sanctuary, the sanctuary and entire Temple were filled with the cloud of the presence of God. Over time, tensions developed because followers of religious rituals forgot the spirit of love and mercy at the heart of the message of God, and things became overritualized. This enraged the prophets, such as Jeremiah, who declared: "The Temple, the Temple! You swear by the Temple, but your acts are abominations. You oppress the stranger, the orphan, and the widow. You shed innocent blood in the Temple." There was a huge gap between the ritual acts and love for the poor! Likewise, the prophet Amos said, "I hate and despise your solemn feasts; I will not listen to the music of your harps. What I long to see is justice flowing like water, and a torrent of righteousness unleashed."

Isaiah, in chapter 58, addresses the issue of ostentatious fasting. He is furious with those who fast with long faces and give the impression that they are holy people obeying the law of God. He speaks God's message:

> Is not this the fast that pleases me: to unloose the thongs of the yoke, to relieve the heavy burden? It is to share your bread with the hungry, to shelter the homeless, and if you see someone naked, to cover them. Then shall your light break forth like the dawn, your wounds will heal speedily, and the glory of God will be with you. If you pray, the Lord your God will respond; you will call, and God will answer, "Here I am." If you remove the chains from among you, if you pour yourself out for the hungry, your light will shine forth in the darkness. God will lead you unceasingly.

What is extraordinary here is that if we open our hearts to the needy and the lonely, it is not just the needy who will be changed, but we will be. We will become like a light, our own wounds will heal quickly, we will be given strength, our health will improve, and God will guide us constantly. This is a message of peace and of love.

Jesus was profoundly inspired by the prophets. The message of peace and love that he shares with them is what we are learning at L'Arche. It is also what John says in his letters: "If you see your brother in need and yet close yourself up, how can the love of God be within you?" We cannot merely recite spiritual words, but we must back them up with acts and deeds of love. Pope Benedict XVI, in his encyclical letter *Deus Caritas Est*, suggests: "If the Eucharist is not translated into concrete gestures of love, it becomes a distorted Eucharist."

With Jesus, the Temple of God, something new has arrived. Jesus is a person. When I go to church and take Communion, it is to meet a person and to be in communion with a person, to be in intimate conversation with him, who himself is in communion with the Father. That communion changes my heart, so that I will open my heart to the friends of Jesus: the poor and the weak.

Today, the same danger that the prophets spoke exists. This danger can enter into Christianity: the danger of wanting to go to religious services and worship but refusing to open our hearts to the poor. Instead of going to church with the desire to have our hearts touched and to be transformed and open to the poor, we can close ourselves off behind the law of rituals and behind a distorted view of the sacred. It is important to allow our hearts to be changed. Isaiah says that our light will break forth like the dawn if we welcome the poor. This welcoming involves relationship. Transformation happens within us, not just when we give money to the poor and needy, but much more profoundly when we enter into a relationship with them. In doing so, we become vulnerable, because it is hard to know how to be in relationship with someone who is in serious need or has no home.

Jesus in the Gospel of Matthew in chapter 25, tells us that at the final judgment we will enter the kingdom of God if we have loved and been compassionate toward those in need. The Lord even says to those who had never met him: "I was naked, and you clothed me. Whatsoever you did to the least of my brothers, you did to me."

At the end of time, the King will say to those who were compassionate toward the hungry and thirsty, the naked and the strangers: "Come, O blessed of my Father, enter the kingdom prepared for you from the foundation of the world, even if you have never known me, because whatever you have done to the least of my brothers, you have done to me."

CHAPTER FIVE

Jesus Meets a Wounded Woman
(JOHN 4:1–30)

Jesus is in Judea, and he wants to return to Galilee with his disciples. He leaves early in the morning, and traveling by foot, he arrives tired, around noon, at the well of Jacob in Samaria.

First, we should have some background information about the Samaritans, because in this Gospel—the Gospel of life, light, and relationship—Jesus is about to meet a Samaritan woman. We are going to witness Jesus living a profound moment of communion with her. In this encounter, we will discover how Jesus wants to meet each one of us.

A Woman of Samaria
The Samaritans and the Jews had been hostile toward each other for about seven hundred years. Like the Jews, the Samaritans were children of Abraham; but they lived in the Northern Kingdom of Israel and had been conquered by the Assyrians, so over time they became cut off from the mainstream of the Jewish religion. These oppressed Samaritans, under Assyrian control, believed only in the first five books of the Bible—not in the books of the prophets, nor in the books of wisdom. Their temple was not in Jerusalem but on Mount Gerizim.

In Jesus's day, the Jews were the majority in Israel, and most of them despised the Samaritans, whose religion they held to be worthless. In the eighth chapter of John, some Pharisees say to Jesus to insult him, "You are a Samaritan, and the devil is in you!" There was no greater insult than this: You are a Samaritan! The Samaritans were considered the lowest of the low. Unfortunately, there are many similar situations around the world and in our different societies today where a people, a group, or a social class considers itself better than others and despises them.

Jesus Is Tired

In John 4, Jesus, tired, sits beside the well. As a human, Jesus is sometimes exhausted, just like all of us. The disciples have gone to buy food. Why did all twelve need to go for food? Maybe they were afraid of the Samaritans and wanted to feel safe as a group in case they were attacked and had to defend themselves. Or perhaps they simply needed to get away from Jesus? Between them and Jesus there must have been many moments of tension, and often they did not understand him. Perhaps they needed to leave him so that they could talk among themselves. Or perhaps they sensed that Jesus needed to be alone.

In any case, Jesus is there, at noon—alone, hot, and tired. A Samaritan woman arrives at the well. We will discover later that she has lived through many broken relationships. People who have been hurt in relationships can be closed in upon themselves. There are recriminations on both sides: against oneself, and against the other. In such a situation, this woman, we can guess, was quite likely closed up in a form of depression.

Normally, women did not come to draw water from the well *at noon*, when it is very hot! Perhaps this woman came to get water then, rather than early in the morning as others did, because she had lived through hurtful experiences, even at the well. Perhaps when she came to the well at the same time as the others, they pointed their fingers at her and laughed: "Woman of ill repute!" She was a wounded woman, hurt by scorn and broken relationships, a woman with a broken self-image. She may have felt unloved and depressed. In this Gospel, we see how Jesus comes close to those who are broken and hurt.

The Vital Need to Be Loved

I try to understand this Gospel through an experience with those who are depressed, wounded, and rejected. I would like to speak to you about Eric, whom I mentioned in chapter four. He was a young man whom we met in a psychiatric hospital, not far from our L'Arche community. He was blind, deaf, and unable to walk. I do not think I have ever met a young person with so much anguish.

Eric had been placed in the psychiatric hospital when he was four years old. His mother was a wonderful woman who had other children. Her husband was a truck driver and was often absent. Unable to cope with Eric alone, she sent him to the psychiatric hospital. She came only once to visit him—she was so upset by what she found there that she never returned.

Was Eric aware of his handicap? I have no idea. Eric did not speak. What I do know is that a newborn baby has a *vital*—I repeat, *vital*—need to be loved. A newborn baby has no means of self-protection and is very fragile and vulnerable. If he is not loved, he is in acute danger because he is defenseless. He needs a mother who will hold him tenderly in her arms and say, "I love you, my beloved child. You are precious to me just as you are." The mother always calls her baby by his name. In this way, a tiny child learns that he is *someone*, because another loves him. If there is nobody to love him, then he is *nobody;* and an intolerable anguish rises up within him.

Anguish is different from fear. If one is afraid of an object, a dog, or something that appears dangerous, and the object or the dog is removed, fear leaves. Anguish is much more existential; it is a sort of inner void: "I am lost; I am nothing, without a center. I do not know who I am. I do not have a place." Little Eric was like that, filled with anguish. He did not know who he was, because he had been abandoned and had experienced many broken relationships.

We welcomed Eric to live with us because the fundamental principle of our L'Arche communities is that of the Gospels: "Every person is sacred." All people, whatever their culture, whatever their capacities or incapacities, whatever their religion, are born of God and are for God. Each person is precious.

What did Eric need when he came to our community? Certainly, he needed professionals. I must say that at L'Arche we have a wonderful team of medical professionals. We worked with a surgeon who operated on Eric's legs, and Eric began to walk. Although a child with severe disabilities needs doctors and other specialists, none of us would want to spend our whole lives with professionals, no matter how competent and sensitive they are! What we each need more fundamentally is friends, brothers and sisters, people who tell us, "I am happy to live with you." We need people who create a family, a community with us. Eric needed that also. He needed in his anguish to meet someone who loved and respected him and created a true relationship with him.

How Do We Approach Those Whose Lives Are Broken?

At the well, Jesus is tired and hot. The Samaritan woman arrives, a woman who, like Eric, has a wounded and broken heart. "Give me something to drink," Jesus asks her. *He* becomes the needy one, putting himself lower than her, saying, "I'm thirsty." He is calling the Samaritan woman to be in the position of giving life to him. Perhaps Jesus is really saying, "I am thirsty for a real relationship."

Here, Jesus is teaching us how to approach people who are fragile and vulnerable like this woman who has a broken self-image. His approach is as a beggar, saying: "I need you." Jesus makes it clear that to approach another from a position of neediness is the way of true compassion, empowering the other. Jesus is not there simply to do good for this woman. Of course, he *will* do her good, but first he wishes to enter into a relationship with her. He wants to meet her, reveal her value, and call her forth. Jesus sees in this woman that which is deep inside her, beyond all the broken relationships of her life, and beyond her feelings of guilt and worthlessness. Jesus sees a woman who is a child of God.

So, Jesus puts himself in a position of inferiority and need with respect to her. He raises her up. She is obviously astounded, because Jews would never talk with a Samaritan! Neither would a single man ever speak with an unaccompanied woman. He is doing something radically countercultural. Astonished, the woman recognizes that this encounter is out of the ordinary. What is happening? "You, a Jew are asking for water from me, a Samaritan woman? Why?"

Jesus answers, "If you knew the gift of God, and who it is asking you for something to drink, I would have given you living water." Extraordinary words! "If you knew the gift of God ..." *We* know that the gift of God is Jesus himself. We have heard this in this Gospel: "God so loved the world that he gave his only Son." Jesus is the gift of God. But the woman is also a gift of God, a woman loved by God. She does not know herself very well. Jesus tells her that if she had known the gift of God, *she* would have asked *him* for water, and he would have given her living water!

"The well is very deep, how will you draw water?" she asks. "Are you greater than our Father Jacob who drew water from this well?" She begins a conversation with him, and even more, she begins to meet him and know him. Bishop Pierre Claverie, a man martyred in his efforts to establish dialogue between Christians and Muslims, once expressed the idea: "Dialogue is important, but meetings are even more important."

Meeting Love

This meeting with the woman of Samaria is very significant at the symbolic level. In Genesis, it is at wells that important biblical people meet their beloved. For instance, Abraham sent his servant to find a wife for his son Isaac. The servant was a bit overwhelmed, wondering, "How will I find someone for him?" He said to himself, "Ah, I have an idea! I will be at the well, and I will say to the first woman who arrives, 'Give me something to drink.' If she responds positively, then she will be the one." That is exactly what happened. Thus, Isaac married Rebecca. Jacob and Rachel also met at a well, as did Moses and Zipphorah. The encounters at wells signify intimate encounters, the birth of mutuality and vulnerability.

Here, we have Jesus coming to the well and saying to the wounded Samaritan woman, "Give me something to drink." This woman is loved by Jesus.

The Promise of Jesus

Jesus next reveals to this broken woman the heart of his message, "If you drink that well water, you will thirst again, whereas if you drink the water that I give you, you will never be thirsty again."

Even if we drink ordinary water regularly, we are thirsty again after a few hours. When we have coffee or tea, we are thirsty again in a little while. But if we do not have enough ordinary water, we die. Water is life-giving. If there is no rain, plants die; if there is no harvest, there is death.

The water that Jesus gives, however, is something else. It symbolizes the Holy Spirit, the Spirit that gives life. Jesus says here the most extraordinary words of the whole Gospel: "The water that I will give will become in the person who drinks it a spring of water welling up to eternal life!"

In the Gospel of John, eternal life signifies the very life of God. One could almost translate the phrase "eternal life" as "the life of the Eternal." Jesus promises this woman, and each one of us, that if we drink the water he gives us, it will become in us a wellspring of the life of the Eternal! If you receive life, you will give life, you will be fecund, and life will flow out through you. If you receive the Holy Spirit, you will give the

Holy Spirit. If you know that you are truly loved, you will be able to love others.

Accepting the Truth of Who We Are

The woman replies, "Give me some of *that* water. Then I will no longer thirst or need to come here to draw water." Jesus responds; he wants to go further in this conversation: "Go, find your husband, and come back here." She says to Jesus, "I have no husband." "Yes, you are right," Jesus replies. "You have no husband. You have lived with five men, and the man you are living with now is not your husband." Jesus delicately reveals to this woman that she is wounded and fragile, having endured many broken relationships. He adds, "What you say is true."

If we are not honest about ourselves, Jesus cannot give us the water that will become in us the source of eternal life. If we believe that we are better than others, if we believe that we do not need to be helped and healed, or if we do not recognize our brokenness and our inner darkness, Jesus cannot give us this living water of eternal life.

Who Is Right and Who Is Wrong?

Then the woman says to Jesus, "I see that you are a prophet!" She then asks what must be the central question in her mind: "Who is right, the Samaritans or the Jews?" Jesus does not respond to this old quarrel. He just says, "Woman, believe me, the hour is coming, and now is upon us, when the true worshippers will worship the Father in the Spirit and in Truth." Through Jesus, the Spirit will be given, and the truth will be revealed. Through Jesus, and in the Spirit, we will enter into a loving relationship with God. Our prayer will take place not only in mountains or temples, but especially in the heart.

The woman responds showing a belief in the coming of the Messiah, "When the Messiah comes he will tell us everything." Jesus replies, "I am he, who speaks to you." Jesus is the Messiah. He looks at her—she who had been rejected and mocked by so many other human beings—with tenderness and love, and he reveals to her his secret. The Samaritan woman is the only person in the Gospel to whom Jesus reveals that he is the Messiah. Transformed by her meeting with Jesus, she goes into the village and calls the people there to meet him.

This Samaritan woman is each of us. The woman symbolizes all of us who have been wounded in our relationships, who have been humiliated, or who have experienced rejection. Jesus comes to meet us and transform us through the gift of the Spirit so that we, too, can give to others the Spirit living in us.

The One I Reject Is the One Who Heals Me

We are all filled with fears, prejudices, and wounds. We are afraid of our own limits, fragility, and mortality. We are afraid of those who are different, of people with disabilities, of people like Eric. If we let go of our defenses, we meet within ourselves those parts of us that are also wounded, disabled, and weak. It is extraordinary to discover within ourselves the wounded person we have been hiding! As we welcome those around us who are wounded, we can enter into a relationship with the wounded person within ourselves. At L'Arche, we have discovered that we are healed by the ones who have been rejected and put aside, as long as we enter into a relationship of mutual vulnerability with them and live a covenant of love with them. They heal us in a mysterious fashion, since they lead us into our deepest being where God resides. It is the presence of Jesus in the wounded that heals the wounds within us and allows us to discover Jesus within us.

We are transformed by those who are weak and rejected, just as this woman was transformed by Jesus. St. Pope John Paul II describes well this teaching power of the weak:

> Disabled people are humanity's privileged witnesses. They can teach everyone about the love that saves us; they can become heralds of a new world, no longer dominated by force, violence and aggression, but by love, solidarity and acceptance, a new world transfigured by the light of Christ, the Son of God who became incarnate, who was crucified and rose for us.[3]

CHAPTER SIX

The Transformation of Faith:
From Generosity to Communion
(JOHN 6:1–71)

The Passover is approaching. Jesus has returned to the mountains around the Lake of Galilee. A multitude of people is following him because they have seen how he has healed so many of the sick.

A Marvelous Picnic

Jesus is seen as a prophet, perhaps even as the Messiah, because of the wonderful things he does. He is touched by this huge crowd of poor people who have followed him—they are tired and hungry. Jesus says to Andrew, "Where will we find food for these people?" Jesus is concerned for the well-being of the people. He cares for them and wants them to be well. Andrew finds a boy who has five loaves of bread and two small fish, but what good is that when the crowd is so large? Jesus says, "Have them sit down."

Then, Jesus takes the five loaves and the two fish, gives thanks, and distributes them. Here we have an extraordinary moment: The bread and fish are multiplied as they are given to each person in this huge and hungry crowd. There is plenty of grass in the area, so people are seated in groups. As Jesus and the disciples give out the bread and the fish, each person receives as much as they need. Everyone is happy, the weather is beautiful, the view of the lake is lovely—all is wonderful!

Then Jesus says, "Pick up all that remains." We know what happened. They collected twelve huge baskets full of leftover fish and bread. This is typical of Jesus. When he does things, he does them with abundance. Remember how in Cana he transformed a huge amount of water into excellent wine? He gives generously, giving more than is required. He gives and gives.

So, the disciples and everyone else are excited. Some say, "Maybe he is the prophet who is to come into the world." I imagine some others murmuring, "To have someone like Jesus as king would be fantastic. We need someone like him to govern us!" Some in the crowd try to seize him to make him king. Imagine having a king who gives bread to everyone and changes water into wine—what a marvel! But Jesus slips away into the mountains. He is not interested in being a king with temporal power. He is to be the king of our hearts, a king of love.

The disciples, probably excited by the success of Jesus, may have been thinking, "More and more people are beginning to believe in him, but now, he has disappeared! What shall we do?"

A Transition in Faith

It is evening. The disciples leave by boat to go to Capernaum, their central gathering point, where both Peter and his mother-in-law lived. They are happy with all that has happened, but also a little worried: Where is Jesus?

Suddenly the wind comes up—quickly, as it can on this lake. The disciples become frightened because a storm is starting. But then they see a light approaching: the face of a man! Now they are even more frightened. They think it must be a ghost. Jesus calls out to them, "It is I! Do not be afraid!" At that moment, their boat touches land; they are saved.

These are the facts written in this Gospel. But the fear the disciples experienced here is also symbolic and reveals something important. We saw that the people on the mountainside were following Jesus because they had seen signs of his power. He had healed many. They thought he must be a great prophet, and they wanted to make him king. When Jesus and the disciples arrive in Capernaum, Jesus wants to speak of something radically new. He says that anyone who eats his flesh and drinks his blood will dwell in him, and he in them. This is startling. This is no longer an "external" Jesus, one who does miracles and is generous to those who pray and ask for favors. This is Jesus who wants to enter into our hearts and live a communion of love with us, to become our intimate friend. Becoming a friend of Jesus, as with any friendship, requires that we leave our own desires and needs to welcome Jesus and live with him. This is huge change implies a transformation—from a relationship with Jesus who is outside of us and whom we can admire, to a relationship with Jesus who lives within us. This change implies a new identity, and for many of us, it requires a radical change of attitude and of heart. Thus, this transformation includes loss; there is fear, an inner storm. But this storm culminates in a new manifestation of Jesus walking on the waters.

Jesus Is the Bread of Heaven

Jesus and his disciples arrive in the middle of the night. The next morning, those who had seen the miracle of the multiplication of the loaves and fishes, who had wanted to seize him to make him king, arrive from the other side of the lake. They ask Jesus, "When did you get here?" Jesus is sad; he can read their hearts. He says, "You are looking for me not because you saw signs but because you have eaten to your fill." They want a miracle but do not want to see the meaning of *the* miracle, to see Jesus as sent by God and as one to be listened to. For Jesus, the miracle reveals who he really is, so that people can believe and follow him and accept his message.

Jesus goes on, "Do not work for food that perishes but for the food that brings eternal life." They ask him, "What is this work of God that we must do?" Jesus replies, "It is to believe, to have faith in him whom God has sent." That is to say, we to have faith in Jesus, and in his message. "But what sign will you do, so that we can see it and believe you? Our fathers ate manna in the desert, which was an obvious sign from God." "It was not Moses who gave you the bread from heaven; my Father gives you the true bread from heaven," Jesus tells them. So they are drawn to Jesus. Like the Samaritan woman who said, "Give me this water," they say to him, "Lord, give us this bread always!"

Jesus helps the people discover the secret he wants to reveal. He says, "I am the bread of life. He who comes to me shall not hunger, and he who believes in me shall never thirst." He wants people to come to him, to trust him, and to believe in him. The people understand when Jesus speaks of bread, because for them the Torah, the books of the prophets, and the books of wisdom—the Word of God—are food, a food necessary to life. Jesus, himself a Jew, knew this well, and it is this insight that he builds on. Jesus is this bread. The prophet Ezekiel had had a vision: When the angel who gave him the scroll with the Word of God said, "Eat!" he ate the whole scroll and said, "It is as sweet as honey." So the people can understand that the Word of God is food.

However, Jesus wants to help them discover progressively that it is not only the Word that is important, but also his body, his real presence. Although the Word is important, his presence is even more so. This is a sensitive point in our time with current communication technologies. People can speak over the Internet, Facebook, and cell phones without actually being present to one another. The idea of presence implies eyes, face, hands, and the body. Our bodies speak even more than the words we say or write.

Jesus comes as the presence of God. The Word became flesh; Jesus reveals through his body his secret of love: "The bread which I will give you is my flesh for the life of the world." The people then begin to murmur. They cannot, or will not, understand. Jesus emphasizes his flesh and says again, "He who eats my flesh and drinks my blood will have eternal life within him." All the work of God is to give life, "the life of God." This is the message of Jesus: that we live of the same life as God. Jesus continues, "He who eats my flesh and drinks my blood I will raise up on the last day." The flesh of Jesus, once entered into our bodies, will lead us to our own resurrection on the last day.

Then there is the key phrase: "He who eats my flesh and drinks my blood dwells in me and I in him." This implies: We will become one, as intimate friends. We will dwell in one another. The word dwell is at the heart of the Gospel. We saw in chapter one that the first two disciples of Jesus asked him, "Where do you dwell?" We will discover that he dwells in the Father and that we are called to dwell in him.

Jesus, on the other shore, had spoken to a multitude who believed in him because of the works he did, because of his generosity and his goodness. He who eats his flesh and drinks his blood will now become his friend. Friendship implies equality: Jesus dwells in me and I in Jesus. We become one. We will work together as one for the glory of the Father. Jesus wants to enter into an intimate relationship with us, which is similar to the intimacy of marriage. It is to live a covenant with Jesus. This had been promised in the Old Testament. The prophet Ezekiel had spoke of this marriage of God with his people. We find it also in the prophet Hosea:

> Therefore I will allure her [the unfaithful wife] and
> speak tenderly to her. I will betroth you to me forever;
> I will betroth you to me in steadfast love and mercy,
> and you will know God.

And there is the beautiful text of Isaiah 62, where God says, "I will give you a new name. You will no longer be called forsaken, but you shall be called 'my delight is in her' … for the Lord delights in you. As the bridegroom rejoices over the bride, so shall your God rejoice over you." So we discover something astonishing: Jesus longs to live in us. He does not wish to give us just grace or a gift of God, nor only a new relationship with God; he wants to fulfill his longing to dwell within us, for the joy of the Father. We are called to be his pleasure and his joy. "As I live through my Father, he who eats me will live through me, and he will live for ever." Jesus desires us to have intimacy with him so that we can give life to the world with and in him.

If Jesus speaks of his flesh as separate from his blood, as he does here, he is anticipating his death, when his blood will be separated from his flesh, though Jesus has not unveiled this yet. We will discover it as we go further into John. It is through this separation of his flesh and his blood that Jesus will give us his life so that we can live and give life.

To live in this intimacy means that we do not seek our own glory, possessions, or power but live and become the desire of Jesus: to be one with his Father and give glory to him. To become the friend of Jesus is to become the friend of God. We might be afraid of that, because it means dying to ourselves. Jesus comes through something tiny, a little piece of bread, consecrated by the priest, which becomes his Body. This is the plan of Jesus. He will leave us physically, but through the bread he will be really present with us. The sacrament becomes a real presence for each one of us; it is not just a moment of grace but a sign of a covenant of love, a friendship offered to us. He is truly present to us and in us.

Many of his disciples, when they hear Jesus, say, "His words are too hard. Who can listen to them?" and they no longer want to be with him. The message of Jesus is certainly beyond us, more than we can imagine. He is challenging all of us to be faithful, to trust even when we do not understand.

This chapter is, in one way, marvelous: It is the revelation of a secret. But it is also terribly sad because people—even Jesus's own disciples—do not want the secret. Maybe many of us do not want to be transformed and find a new identity. I imagine that the twelve who had been chosen by Jesus were also feeling lost. All was going so well, and many people were beginning to follow Jesus—it was wonderful! And now with these words about his flesh and his blood, people were leaving. The twelve must have been in a state of shock.

Then Jesus turns toward them, with their anxious faces: "You also, are you going to leave me?" I can almost hear the tears in his voice as he says this. Then Peter cries out, "To whom shall we go?" Even in this phrase, "To whom shall we go?" there is a mild hesitation. It is an affirmation of faith, nonetheless, and Peter adds, "You have the words of eternal life, and we believe that you are the Holy One of God." Peter's is a statement of deep trust. He will stay even in the face of words that are too hard.

Jesus then reveals something that profoundly wounds him, a broken communion. He realizes that Judas has lost trust in him. Thus, this chapter, which had started so marvelously with a multitude of people following Jesus, ends sadly because so many are leaving Jesus. Judas no longer believes. However, the eleven stay and believe. They are going to be the guardians of this extraordinary gift of the body of Jesus, a gift to be shared, a gift to lead us into an intimate friendship with Jesus.

CHAPTER SEVEN

Walls That Destroy Trust in Jesus

(JOHN 7:1–39; 8:12–59; 9:1–34)

In Capernaum, Jesus revealed his secret: He so loves human beings that he wants to be a real presence to them, to give his flesh to be eaten, and to dwell in them. Many people could not accept this and turned away from him.

Following the Gospel of John, we next find ourselves back in Jerusalem. It is the Feast of Tents, an extraordinary festival, a feast of light and of water. It is a great celebration in Jerusalem. Light and lamps are everywhere. It is extraordinarily beautiful!

The Cry of Jesus

For the Feast of the Tents, people would come out of their houses to live in roughly made tents built from branches. Why? It called to their minds their sojourn from Egypt and reminded them that they were pilgrims, always walking toward God.

Jesus had said that he would not attend the festival, but in the end, he goes. He begins teaching in the Temple. People discuss what he is saying. Some support him; others stand in opposition, saying that he is leading the crowd astray. One can sense the tension. Suddenly, on the last day of the festival, the big day, Jesus stands and cries out, "Whoever is thirsty, let him come to me and drink!"

Can you imagine? In the middle of that huge crowd, Jesus stands and cries out, "Whoever is thirsty, let him come to me and drink!" It is as if the heart of Jesus is bursting. He cannot stand all the bickering about where he comes from and all the rest. These words are as surprising and shocking as when he spoke of his flesh to be given and eaten in order that we may have life.

The cry of Jesus flows from his passionate and loving desire to liberate people from slavery and give them life. John says that God so loved the world that he sent his only beloved Son to give life—and the Son gives life by living with people and in them. He offers a friendship with them, and this friendship implies deep respect for them, respect for their inner freedom. Jesus is proclaiming the mystery of the love of God that we read in Isaiah 55: "Come, come, all you who are thirsty and hungry. Come and drink! Come and eat!"

We also find this life-giving image of Jesus in the extraordinary vision of Ezekiel. In Ezekiel 47, the prophet describes a vision of the new Temple. We have already spoken of the new Temple as the body of Jesus. In the vision of Ezekiel, water flows out of the right side of the Temple, and as it continues to flow, it gives life to all. The fish come alive, and the water continues to pour out. The water rises and gives life. The leaves of the trees that grow on each side of the water heal the sick. This vision reflects the reality that Jesus is thirsty to give life and wants people in turn to thirst for life and for his love. Jesus is this new Temple from which flow rivers of life for all those who are thirst for them.

After having said, "Whoever is thirsty, let him come to me and drink!" Jesus says, "From the breast of the one who believes in me, as Scripture says, rivers of living waters will flow." Rivers of living waters will flow from the heart of the one who has trust in Jesus and believes in him! This, of course, reminds us of what Jesus had said to the Samaritan woman: "The water that I will give will become in the person who drinks it a spring of water welling up to eternal life!" So, the water that Jesus gives us will become in us a wellspring or a fountain that gives life to others. Through the Spirit we have received, we can transmit the Spirit. Waters will flow forth from each of us to give life, if we trust Jesus and thirst for the living waters that only he can give us.

The mission of Jesus is to announce the Good News to the poor, to help the poor discover their value, stand up, find their dignity, and grow in love. Jesus has chosen us to live his mission. He wants our hearts to be wellsprings of living water, loving people and helping them achieve their goals. Thus, when we announce the Good News to the poor, it is not to tell them, "Jesus loves you," but rather to say, "*I* love you. I commit myself to you in the name of Jesus."

Walls Are Founded on Fear

In modern Bethlehem, a huge wall has been built to separate Palestine and the state of Israel. Walls such as these are painful; walls are founded on fear. In this eighth chapter of the Gospel of John, especially after Jesus has spoken about being a fountain of life, there are tensions. People do not want to listen to Jesus. There are walls in their hearts that prevent them from listening to him. Is it because they fear him?

In the third chapter of Genesis, Adam and Eve, after being tempted by the serpent, rejected God. They wanted to do their own thing, to decide their own future and do what they thought was good for them. God, however, came looking for them: "Adam, where are you?" Adam replied, "I was afraid because I was naked, and so I hid."

Here we see three things: fear, nakedness, and hiding. We hide behind walls because we are frightened. What is this nakedness? It is our fragility, our powerlessness; it is all our human poverty. We close our hearts to each other in self-protection and hiding. We are frightened of revealing our weakness.

St. Francis of Assisi

Francis of Assisi said that he felt repulsed by those who were suffering from leprosy. In the Middle Ages, there were some twenty thousand leprosariums in Europe. He was disgusted; he did not want to be close to them. We can understand that because of the deformed faces of such people and the smell characteristic of the disease. Francis was therefore shocked and afraid and turned away from them. Then one day Francis said, "The Lord led me toward them, and I served them, and when I left I felt a new gentleness in my body and in my spirit." When the walls of fear fall down, we can begin to meet each other and discover the vulnerable and wounded heart of the other.

We see such healing meetings in our L'Arche communities with regard to people with disabilities. Young people (age fifteen or so) from local schools come to spend a day with us that, of course, includes meeting people with disabilities. After their visit, they complete an evaluation of their short stay. Many say, "Before coming to L'Arche I was very frightened." They were frightened of people with disabilities because they are different. In our world, so many people are frightened of others who are of a different culture, religion, or social class.

Several years ago, I had the privilege of visiting Chile. On the road from the airport, my driver told me, "On the left are the slums, and on the right are the houses of the rich. Nobody crosses this road. Nobody." The poor are frightened of the rich, and the rich are frightened of the poor. There is no meeting between the two. The road is like a wall. We live in a world where we create walls because of our fears. Walls can surround our hearts when we are frightened of others.

Jesus Is the Light of the World

Chapter eight of John's Gospel begins with Jesus saying, "I am the light of the world, and whoever follows me will not walk in darkness, but will have the light of life."

Jesus did not come to take away our fears, but he gives us a new strength through the Holy Spirit, so that we are not governed by fear, nor live in darkness. Jesus cries out that whoever follows him will not be lost but will find the way. He will have the light of life. What is this light? It is the light that flows from love and to life. It is the wisdom of love. The vision of Jesus is a vision of unity: bringing people into communion with one another, breaking down walls that separate people. What is it that gives us the strength to accept our weaknesses and fears, and not to hide behind a wall? How can we accept that we are unique and important, and that we do not need to fall into what the "tyranny of normality" and be like everyone else? The solution is to follow Jesus, and be with him.

Tension mounts, and at one moment Jesus says, "I come from above, and you are from below. You are of the world; I am not of the world." It is as if he is saying, "You cannot understand what I bring, because I am from God."

"They ask him, "Who are you?" and Jesus responds, "When you have lifted up the Son of Man, you will know that I am." You will know, not *who* I am, but *that* I am! This is the name of God.

To understand these words, *I am*, that define who Jesus is, it is necessary to go back to the third chapter of Exodus. This is a key chapter in the whole of the Bible. It is about the burning bush. Moses had an encounter with God, and he heard God say, "I have seen the misery of my people, and I will send you to Pharaoh that you may bring forth my people to liberate them."

Then Moses said, "When I return to the Israelites, they will ask me, 'What is the name of God?'" God responded, "I am who I am." He added, "Tell the Israelites that 'I am' has sent me to you." I AM. Jesus is existence; God is existence. He is the whole truth. As for the rest of us, I exist, we all exist, but some years ago we did not exist. In the future we will no longer exist in the same way. Jesus, however, *is* existence. Now we have the true revelation of Jesus who is God, the Son of God. He is; he is the truth.

The Truth Will Set You Free

"If you dwell in my word (*logos*), you will truly be my disciples, and you will know the truth, and the truth will make you free."

What does this mean? Here are some examples:

Mother Teresa, an Albanian nun, went against the current that makes people see extreme poverty—even people dying in the streets—as normal and who therefore do nothing about it. She spent her life in service to the poorest of the poor in India.

Martin Luther King, Jr., an American pastor, went against the current, persuasively speaking against racial prejudice and social injustice. He was free and spoke out and was later assassinated.

Anna Politkovskaya was a Russian journalist from Moscow. She was free. She spoke out against the war in Chechnya and against the Russian president. When she survived an attempt to poison her, she was shot to death.

To be true is to be free to say the truth, even when people do not want to hear the truth. Many are afraid of the truth; they are afraid of going against the current. They are afraid to speak out.

Slaves of Others' Desires

In chapter eight, Jesus tells the Jewish authorities that they are slaves. The Jewish authorities say, "We? We are nobody's slaves. We are free. We are the children of Abraham." Jesus explains that there is the slavery of sin, of fear, of compulsions, of the ego, which can make us want to prove that we are better than others. There is also the slavery of normality and many other forms of slavery.

The Jewish authorities then become more and more angry, "You have the devil in you." Jesus continues, asserting with strength, "He who believes in me will never die." The Jewish authorities respond, "You are greater than our father Abraham who died?" Jesus answers, "Before Abraham was, *I am.*" Jesus preexisted. He is the Son of God. Jesus is free, and he speaks the truth. If we dwell in his word, we too will be free.

The Truth Is Reality

In chapter nine, we see a young man who is blind healed by Jesus. The authorities are imprisoned in (confined by) an ideology—an intellectual theory cut off from reality and experience. If we become trapped in an ideology, we refuse to accept reality. We refuse to accept others because we are closed up in our own ideas and certitudes. Jesus came to liberate us from ideology.

This young man who had been born blind and who was healed by Jesus becomes a disciple of Jesus, throwing himself at his feet, saying, "Lord, I believe." He believes in Jesus, who is the liberator. The blind man speaks the truth about his healer; he is free—but the authorities throw him out from the synagogue.

Jesus is calling each of us not to hide behind the walls that give us security but to be free, free to be ourselves and to speak the truth, even if it hurts.

Jesus Teaches Us to Be Shepherds
(JOHN 10: 1–21)

Until now, Jesus has been revealing his love for people. In the sixth chapter, he announces his secret, his desire to live in each one through the gift of his Body and of his Blood. At the Feast of Tents, we saw him crying out, "He who is thirsty, come to me and drink!" While he is still at the Feast of Tents, now we are entering into the chapter of the true shepherd.

Jesus reveals himself as the Good Shepherd. In reality, the word good is not exactly correct. In Greek the word is *kalos*, meaning "fine, noble, or beautiful." Perhaps the best translation would be "the *true* shepherd." Maybe we are not familiar with shepherds, but we may be familiar with the concept of servant leadership. This chapter is about authority.

Jesus Is the True Shepherd
Jesus reveals himself as the shepherd of a flock who is filled with an extraordinary love and tenderness. Throughout the Old Testament, God is revealed as the shepherd of his people, the Jewish people. For example, Isaiah 40 tells of a messenger of the Lord who will reveal the Messiah: "Here is your God, like a shepherd who carries the lambs on his breast" (Isaiah 40:11). What tenderness!

Jesus is the true shepherd because he is the Lamb of the Father. To be the one who truly leads and guide others, one must know how to obey. Jesus, the Lamb of God, is at the same time the Beloved Son, and the one who will shepherd his flock.

He will call forth a people, and this people will be the Church, all who believe and trust in him. Jesus says, "I am the true Shepherd. I know my sheep and my sheep know me, as the Father knows me and I know the Father; and I will lay down my life for the sheep." There is an exquisite tenderness here. Jesus loves his flock so much that he is in communion with them and will even give his life for them. We will discover that Jesus the Shepherd has a personal relationship with each one in his flock.

The Primary Role of the Shepherd

The image of Jesus as a shepherd is suggested by the prophet Ezekiel. Speaking through his prophet, God strongly condemns false shepherds who look after themselves and do not care for the sheep. The true shepherd cares for the weakest ones. This is what Ezekiel declared, in the name of God: "I myself will be the shepherd of my sheep, and I myself will make them lie down, says the Lord. I will seek the lost, I will bring back the strayed, I will bind up the wounded, and I will strengthen the weak" (Ezekiel 34:13–16). Jesus fulfills the prophecy of Ezekiel.

The primary role of the shepherd is to be with, to watch over, and to care for little ones, especially the most fragile. The shepherd is similar to a mother. A mother is called to be a shepherdess who loves her little ones, saying: "I love you, and I am always in communion with you." She watches over the littlest one with all his or her fragilities and vulnerabilities. Many of us have lived a beautiful relationship with our parents, but others may have felt unloved or even rejected. The authority that Jesus teaches us is an authority that calls people to freedom and to life.

The Qualities of a Shepherd

Jesus in speaking about himself as the true shepherd is also teaching each of us how to become true shepherds. Each one of us—parents, teachers, priests and ministers, and all who are responsible for the growth of others—have a lot to learn about exercising authority through a spirit of service, helping people grow toward greater inner freedom and maturity.

First of all, Jesus says that the shepherd has a clear responsibility. He does not jump over the wall, into the enclosure where the sheep are gathered to be kept for the night. Instead, he enters by the door opened up by the night watchman. He has a mandate, a recognized authority. He is clearly responsible for those under him.

Jesus also shows us the most important role of a shepherd: to know each sheep by its name. In the Bible, one's name is something very important. The shepherd knows each one by name and is in communion with each one.

What is this communion with each sheep? It is to know and love each one and to be concerned for the welfare and growth of each one. The shepherd loves his people, his flock. He loves each one personally, and he knows each by his or her name. To know people by name is to know their gifts, their mission, their weaknesses, and maybe their history. Each one of us has a history, a beautiful history, but also a history of fragility and of pain that has modified us. The heart of the relationship of the shepherd with his sheep is a relationship of trust. He knows his sheep; the sheep know him. They are bonded in mutual trust. All this takes time. It means that the shepherd has a welcoming heart and knows how to listen, not just with his or her head, but with all he or she is.

What is it that the shepherd wants? What does a mother or a father as a good shepherd want? They want their children to become themselves as individual persons, to grow in inner freedom to greater life. They respect their child deeply, and they respect his or her vocation and mission as the child grows to be fully human. There is a danger for parents to want to possess or control their children, to want them to be "a success" in society, to become "somebody," rather than letting their children find their deeper happiness freely. There is also a danger for parents to let children just do and have whatever they want; they may have no vision for education. Children can then grow up controlling their parents. To be a shepherd, especially with little ones, one must be very present to love children, to guide them, and to awaken their consciences in order to help them grow free in trust, in love, and in a sense of responsibility and of justice.

In my own life, I had a deep experience of this. When I was thirteen years old, I was living in Canada, and there grew within me a desire to join the British Navy, which meant journeying to England. This was in 1942, and one in five ships were then being sunk by German submarines in the Atlantic. I went to see my father, and I asked him if I could join the navy.

He asked me several questions and tried to dissuade me, but I affirmed my desire. I will always remember what he said, "I trust you, and if you want to do it, you must do it."

It was only much later that I realized that that had been my initiation into adulthood. I had been able to leave the family with my parents' blessing and travel alone in a troopship to enter the officers' training school. My father had said, "I trust you." Since he had trusted me, I could trust myself, my intuitions, my longings, and my conscience. I also believe that his trust in me helped me to trust others.

Flowers turn naturally toward the light; they turn toward the sun. Children are drawn to the light: the light of truth, the light of justice, and, of course, the light of love. They know when they are loved and trusted. It is, of course, important to teach that there are laws. There are limits that are indispensable for a child to understand and to live. Most important, however, is that children, knowing they are loved and trusted, develop confidence in themselves, in their own personal conscience toward trust, love, and justice, and that they discover their own personal path to inner freedom.

Jesus says that the shepherd leads the sheep out of the enclosure. He goes before them, and the sheep follow him because they know his voice. They trust the true shepherd. Psalm 23 says that the Lord leads his sheep to lie down near green pastures; he leads them to still waters, and he restores their soul; he leads them in the path of justice and truth.

Jesus, through his love and his example, leads us to the Father, to the God of compassion and forgiveness. A shepherd is called to lead people to spiritual and intellectual nourishment, to those places and people who will give them the desire to grow in love, in truth, and in freedom. Jesus leads people so that they may discover the heart of his message: to announce the Good News to the poor. This means we are not only to tell the poor, "You are loved by God," but also to say to each one, "I love you, and in the name of Jesus, I commit myself to you." The shepherd leads people to open up to others, to become responsible for others, to transmit life.

Avoiding the Double Message

Shepherds must avoid giving a double message. Here's an example. I was asked to visit with and question some young people in Quebec who had been involved with drugs. There were four or five of them aged sixteen to eighteen. I asked them what they had experienced in living with drugs, what it had brought them, and so on. Then I asked them, "What was the reaction of your parents when they learned you were taking drugs?" All of them said, "They were very angry." So I asked them, "What was your reaction to the anger of your parents?" Then one of them looked at me and said in anguish, "Sir, my father is an alcoholic!" He was saying: What right has he to tell me not to take drugs when he himself is an alcoholic? If the father of that young man had been able to say to him, "Do not do as I have done, for as you see, I am an alcoholic, and I have hurt your mother and all you children. I suggest you stop using drugs," this would not have been a double message; this would have been the truth. To speak the truth we must live the truth. A shepherd leads by example, an example of being fulfilled and happy and filled with truth.

To lead is to be consistent with who we are and what we live. To have faith and to trust is not just for when all is going well but also for difficult moments. It is easy to trust when the wind is behind the sails; it is more difficult when there are trials and hardships, or when we are laughed at or seen as weird, or when there are problems in relationships. Trusting during those moments of difficulty is what transmits faith. Children see double messages very quickly; they can sense immediately anything that smells of hypocrisy, when words and life do not match.

Recognizing One's Own Weaknesses

To be a good shepherd is also to recognize one's own weaknesses and mistakes. Sometimes parents, institutions, priests, and all of us in positions of responsibility, for a multitude of reasons, make mistakes like everyone else. We can hurt people sometimes without even realizing it. We can do wrong and be unjust. It is important to recognize our errors and ask for forgiveness.

When a child is born, the mother and father are a bit like God. The child is fed, nourished, and given everything by their parents, even their existence.

However if parents commit injustices or accuse children of having done something that they have not done, then the child is deeply wounded. There can be a break in their faith in God when they see their parents doing things that are unjust, without asking forgiveness. Shepherds or servant leaders are called to be models of forgiveness, models also who admit their weakness and vulnerability and their need for help.

I myself have sometimes lived through difficulties in L'Arche. When I left as community director, I spent a year at the foyer of La Forestiere, where Lucien lived. Lucien had a serious catatonic psychosis: He could not look anyone in the eye. He did not speak, nor could he walk. He had spent thirty years with his mother, a wonderful woman who coped with all his crises and his gestures. She knew how to respond to his cry. Eventually Lucien's mother fell ill and had to spend time in the hospital. Lucien was put into another hospital, where he suffered terrible anguish. Anguish is the result of a broken relationship. Lucien screamed and screamed because he was separated from the only person in the world who loved him. Finally Lucien came to our community, and I had the privilege of living with him for a year. When he screamed, sometimes for two hours or more, it awoke something very deep within me. I would even say that his anguish evoked my own anguish. I felt waves of anger rise up within me, anger that could easily have turned into hate and violence.

We are all capable of doing harm; we all need to ask forgiveness. I do not think that Lucien understood. Several years later at the time of his death, I remember being close to his dead body and saying to him, "Forgive me, Lucien. You really taught me something important about myself." Lucien taught me about who I am and what I need to work on in myself. Shepherds should not only help others to grow; they also are called to grow in a love that is wise. We are human beings each with our own fragilities, and each with our own secrets, gifts, or talents. The shepherd is called to recognize both his fragilities and his secrets, and to help others live their own secrets.

Claudia taught me about living our talents. She lived in our community in Honduras, in Suyapa, near Tegucigalpa. She was autistic and blind. She rarely spoke any word. She was strikingly beautiful and delicate. I recall that one day, when I was sitting across from her at table, I asked her in Spanish, "Claudia, why are you so happy?" She replied after quite a long pause, "God." When Claudia says one word, there is no need to ask another question! One word from Claudia is verbose! Afterward, I went to see Nadine, who had founded the community, and I said, "Did you hear what Claudia said?" Nadine said she had. "How do you interpret her response?" I asked. She said, "It's her secret." We each have a secret in the depth of our beings, in union with God and with others. The good shepherd is called to respect that secret within each one and help that secret to grow and to deepen.

To Become a Shepherd Like Jesus

To become a good shepherd, we are called to become like Jesus and care deeply for the people we are responsible for. We are not just salaried personnel; it is not just a job we are doing. We are called to help people to grow to greater human and Christian maturity. Jesus, the source of life, calls us each of us to become a source of life as well. Jesus, who is the Light of the world, also calls each of us, his disciples, to become a light for the world. We are called to become true shepherds, like Jesus, with all his tenderness and capacity for forgiveness, with his capacity to help people to raise up; and for this we need the Holy Spirit. If we are to become shepherds like Jesus and give our lives, we need to have our hearts of stone transformed into hearts of flesh; we need to receive the Holy Spirit. Since we have God's help to be good shepherds, it is also necessary to be good sheep. We must ourselves be obedient to the Holy Spirit and to our community in order to aid others to become fully themselves in their mission in the Church.

CHAPTER NINE

The One You Love Is Sick: Lazarus
(JOHN 11:1–54; 12:1–11)

The Gospel of John takes us today into a little family in Bethany, some three to four miles from Jerusalem. We have already heard of this family in the Gospel of Luke, when Jesus came to eat with Martha and Mary. There was tension then between these two sisters.

Martha is a practical, busy woman doing the cooking; Mary is more sensitive, more affective, and more loving. She is on her knees before Jesus, drinking his words. Martha is irritated, "Tell her to come and help me!" Jesus answers, "Mary has chosen the better place."

Lazarus: The Friend of Jesus

Let us now return to this text of John's Gospel. It starts with the two sisters who send a message to Jesus, who is a two days' journey away: "The one you love is sick." This is an astonishing message! It is a beautiful way to speak of their brother—"the one you love." It is clear that Jesus is part of this family. John himself says, "Jesus loved Martha and Mary and Lazarus." There are bonds between them. Here, Jesus does not call Lazarus to follow him, but it is Lazarus calling Jesus. This is something new! Jesus probably often would come there to rest; he feels comfortable with this little family.

But who is this Lazarus? We are going to learn that he does not speak in the Gospels, but several times Jesus's love for him is mentioned. At one point Jesus says, "Our friend Lazarus." He lives with two unmarried sisters, which seems strange in the culture of that time.

I personally have a feeling—that comes, perhaps, from my life in L'Arche—that Lazarus has a disability, perhaps a severe one, and that Jesus often comes to be with him. In this way we can understand why the two unmarried sisters would call Jesus to come to be with Lazarus: "The one you love is sick." However, Jesus waits, and when he finally arrives, he is too late. Lazarus is dead.

Martha and Mary Go to Meet Jesus

When Jesus arrived in Bethany, Martha comes running and throws herself at his feet. She says something that appears slightly critical, "Lord, if you had been here, my brother would not have died. Even now I know whatever you ask from God, God will give you."

Jesus responds, "Your brother will rise up!"

"I know he will rise up, but in the resurrection on the last day," Martha replies

"I am the resurrection and the life, and if someone believes in me, he will not die; do you believe this?"

"Yes! Lord, I believe that you are the Christ, the Son of God, who is coming into the world."

Martha is a woman of faith. This is an explosion of her faith, a little like Peter's when he said, "You are the Christ."

She returns to the house and whispers to Mary, "The Master has arrived, and he is calling for you." Mary, surrounded by her friends and neighbors who have been weeping and grieving with her, runs to Jesus and throws herself at his feet: "Lord, if you had been here, my brother would not have died." Jesus does not respond. But John says that when Jesus sees Mary weeping and all her friends weeping, he is deeply disturbed in his spirit and anguished. He says, "Where have you put him?" And then, it is said that "Jesus wept." Yes, Jesus shed tears for his friend.

The Emotion of Jesus

What is happening here? Jesus is deeply disturbed in his spirit, anguished, and weeping. What is this deep emotion that Jesus is living? It seems he is passing through a sort of crisis. Is it just tears in front of death, or is it something else?

We will read later that, after the resurrection of Lazarus, many people will begin to believe in Jesus. Others go to Jerusalem and tell the high priest, "He has just resurrected a dead man, and all the people are starting to believe in him." So Caiaphas, a little panicked, calls the grand council of the Jews—the Sanhedrin—to assemble. Together they make the decision that Jesus should be eliminated, "because if he continues, everyone will flock to him, and the Romans will take control over our country and our holy place." It is decided: Jesus must die.

Jesus, in front of Mary, must know that if he resurrects Lazarus, it will be the last straw. The Jewish authorities will want to get rid of him quickly. If he brings Lazarus to life, it will mean his death. This moment of Jesus's tears and anguish, then, is a moment of deep and mysterious emotion. He is moved by the tears of Mary with whom he is deeply bonded.

And he is moved by the terrible reality of his own passion if he raises Lazarus from the dead.

Lazarus, Come Out!

Jesus, deeply disturbed in his spirit, goes toward the tomb. "Remove the stone," he directs them.

"But he has been dead for four days; the stench is terrible," says Martha.

"Do you not know that, if you believe, you will see the glory of God?" The glory of God—that is, who God is, the love of God, the power of God.

At that moment, Jesus turns around and prays, "Father, I thank you for granting what I ask, as you always do. I pray not for my own sake, but for those who are here, that they may believe that you have sent me." He turns to the tomb: "Lazarus, come out!" The dead man emerges, tottering. Jesus simply says, "Unbind him, and let him go."

Did Mary throw herself into the arms of Jesus, or into the arms of her brother Lazarus? It is a profoundly emotional moment, one of great beauty.

Jesus Calls Each of Us to Arise

As always with John, there is the event, and then there is the symbolism. There is a real event: Jesus raises a man from the dead. Maybe the great prophet Ezekiel can help us understand the symbolism of this event. He is a prophet who has great visions and dreams; he may even be considered a "wild" prophet.

In one dream, Ezekiel sees a valley, a huge valley, full of dry bones. Maybe it is a sort of nightmare. He hears the Lord

God, who asks him, "Son of Man, can these bones live?" (Ezekiel 37:1–14). If God ever asks you such a question, try to respond as Ezekiel did: "Only you, Lord, know." So the Lord God said to him, "Then, prophesy." And so, Ezekiel prophesies. Then all the bones begin to arrange themselves one upon another. However, the bones are not yet living people; they are merely bones covered over with skin and nerves. They are like stone figures. The Lord God repeats again, "Prophesy, prophesy!" And Ezekiel prophesies again, and *life* begins to enter the bones. Behold, the valley of dead bones, dried up and brittle, has now become a huge group of men and women standing together!

That is the vision, the dream, and afterward the dream must be interpreted to understand its meaning. The interpretation must come from God. In Ezekiel we read:

> Son of Man, these bones are the whole house of Israel who had been exiled to Babylon. They are all saying, "Our bones are dried up, our hope is destroyed, and we are clean cut off." That is why you will prophesy to them: This is what the Lord your God says to you, "I will open your tombs, I will lead you out of your tombs, O my people, and I will lead you back to the soil of Israel. You will know that I am God when I open your tombs, O my people. I will put my Spirit in you, and you will live! I will establish you on your soil, and you will know that I, God, have spoken and I have done it, says the Lord." (Ezekiel 37:11–14)

Extraordinary! This utterance, hundreds of years before Jesus, to a desperate people—a people whose bones are dry and brittle, whose hope is destroyed—is also about us, when we feel all dried up. We receive these words today, as a people who are engulfed in all sorts of crises: wars, financial crises, ecological crises. They echo our anguish that all is over, finished, hopeless. But then it is revealed! There is the plan of God, the vision of God, and the wisdom of God. The wisdom of God is this: "I will lead you out of your tombs of despair, O my people, and I will put my spirit in you."

To Be Free to Love

What is the tomb? We, as human beings, have memory, and we can each ask ourselves: What are our earliest memories? Perhaps we can remember how we were when we were five or six years old, though we may not be able to go farther back. All these early years of our lives about which we can remember nothing are a bit like a tomb. It is as if there were a stone blocking the entrance to this tomb. What is in this tomb? I remember a psychoanalyst telling me, "The body remembers everything." The intellectual memory cannot remember, but the body remembers all that has happened, sometimes even what happened in the mother's womb. So of these hidden memories are the traumas, fears, abandonment, or other impossible situations that children have lived. They can be too terrible for them to speak of.

So, hidden within each of us there is a place that is like a tomb, to which we do not have access. In that place there are the elements of death: our fears and traumas. We human beings are made in an extraordinary way. All that has happened to us since our birth, even before our birth, is locked away there— including these fears that can be destabilizing.

For example, one man as a child suffered the death of his twin brother, when they were both in the womb of their mother, but nobody ever talked to him about this death. He grew up living in a terrible fear of death, without understanding why. This obsessive fear of death developed because nobody had ever spoken with him about what happened to his brother in the womb.

Fears are there, hidden in the tomb, influencing and controlling our lives and attitudes. Jesus wants us to become free—not to be governed and manipulated by fears and terrible anguishes and insecurities. He wants us to be men and women of freedom.

So, this text of Lazarus brings each of us back to the tomb within, where anguish dwells. Jesus does not want to set us free. He will not always take away our insecurities, but he will give us a new force to accept them, to become conscious of them, and to live with them: "I will put my Spirit in you." Jesus wants to put his Spirit in us, so that we will no longer be men and women driven by fear, but free people, free to love.

Mary Anoints the Feet of Jesus

Lazarus is alive, risen from the dead, and many people are beginning to believe in Jesus because of this miracle. Others go to see the high priest in Jerusalem, a few kilometers from Bethany. There, the high priest, Caiaphas, calls together the Sanhedrin, and together they decide that Jesus must be eliminated, and also to get rid of Lazarus.

Sometime later, maybe a week, Jesus arrives back in Bethany. He is on his way to Jerusalem for the Feast of the Passover. There must have been tension within him; he knows he is going to his death. Jesus and his disciples take a meal in Bethany at the house of Simon the leper. We know nothing of this man, except that he was a leper, an outcast. In the Gospel of John, there are many important meals. Meals are important for Jesus; they are places of friendship, where friendship is expressed and celebrated.

During the meal, Martha is serving. We remember that Jesus loved Martha, Mary, and Lazarus. We also remember the intimate bond between Lazarus and Jesus: "the one you love." The one Jesus loves is at his side.

At one moment during the meal, Mary enters the room with a little bottle of precious nard oil, worth about three hundred denarii—that is, about the equivalent of a year's salary for a workman. She anoints the feet of Jesus with this precious oil and then unties her hair and starts to dry the feet of Jesus! We are told that the room was filled with the extraordinary scent of the perfume.

Remember how several days earlier Jesus had said, "Remove the stone," and Martha had protested saying, "But he is dead four days, and the stench will be terrible." Then there was the odor of death, and now there is this new odor of love. This gesture of Mary was shocking. Perhaps this is why when Matthew and Mark were talking about it later, they reported that she had poured the oil on his *head*—how a king is anointed. This would sound more acceptable. However, John says she poured this precious ointment, not on his head, but on his feet, and she dried them with her hair. It is a gesture that is shocking, but it is also exquisitely beautiful.

In the Gospel of Luke, it is said that when Jesus had seen how the most simple people received the Word of God, he was so thrilled that he quivered with joy. He cried, "Blessed are you Father, Lord of heaven and earth, for having hidden these things from the intellectuals and the powerful, and revealed them to little ones!" (Luke 10:21). The heart of Jesus must have quivered with joy also at this gesture of love by Mary.

Judas, on the other hand, seems to be like those intellectuals who do not understand. He criticizes Mary: "This oil could have been sold and the money given to the poor" (John 12:1–11). John adds that Judas himself was dishonest and a thief.

Is there something else going on here as well? Could it be that perhaps Judas and the other men do not understand the special bond between Jesus and Mary? There is an intimacy between them; their relationship is unique, very different from the relationship of the disciples with Jesus. At some moments the disciples discuss who among them is the most important, the greatest. Perhaps there is also a sort of jealousy between the disciples and Mary. This misunderstanding still exists in the Church today around the relationship between men and women.

What is touching is the way in which Jesus reacts to the criticism of Judas. He comes to the defense of Mary: "Leave her alone. She has done something beautiful to prepare for my burial. I will not always be with you, but the poor you will always have with you" (John 12:7–8). In Matthew, Jesus's defense of Mary is even stronger: "Everywhere in the world where this Gospel will be proclaimed, what this woman has done will also be proclaimed" (Matthew 26:13). When Jesus defends a friend who has been criticized, he comes out very strong. Mary will be known by everybody in the world!

What is Jesus telling us here? This confrontation with Judas seems to speak to a tension that still exists today between wealth used in churches—for beautiful vestments for the liturgy, for golden chalices, and so on—and the misery and hunger of the poor. Perhaps Jesus is telling us: "Yes, I will not always be with you physically as I am now, but I will *always* be present with you in the poor."

Remember Lawrence, the deacon of the third century who led all the poor of the streets to the Roman authorities, who wanted to get hold of all the riches of the Church. He said, "The riches of the Church are the poor." Is Jesus also telling us that?

This scene with Mary anointing the feet of Jesus is beautiful! Mary gives her all to Jesus. Since this perfume was so expensive, it was probably her most valuable possession. She gives everything, and in doing so she reveals her heart. She knows that Jesus listened to her tears by raising her brother from the dead. She knows also that because he listened to her tears and acted upon them, he is condemned to death. Jesus had also given everything. He knows it now, and she knows it as well. He is now moving toward his death. Thus, in response to Jesus' total gift of self, Mary gives him a total gift of self. Mary is an example for us, as disciples of Jesus; we, too, are to give our all to follow Jesus, to be with him, and to trust him.

The disciples are still caught up in respectability and questions of money. Mary has only one desire: to love Jesus and to be for him a source of consolation. The disciples do not understand that Jesus is moving toward rejection and humiliation. Mary seems to understand. Jesus is touched by her audacious love.

CHAPTER TEN

Jesus: The Path of Peace
(JOHN 12:12–50)

Jesus leaves Bethany. Mary has just bathed his feet with the precious oil. In descending the several miles that lead to Jerusalem, the perfume must still be on his feet. Perhaps even more deeply, the perfume of the love of Mary embalms his heart. He has felt understood, accepted, and loved.

He leaves, but he already knows that he will be killed. As he approaches Jerusalem, people acclaim him: "Hosanna! Hosanna! Son of David, king of Israel!" They are waving palm branches. However, Jesus knows that many of those shouting will perhaps in a few days have a different cry: "Crucify him! Crucify him!" This is the point at which John recites the text of Zechariah, which unveils something new about Jesus and his mission of peace. Here then is the text of Zechariah, the first part of which is cited by John:

> Rejoice greatly, O daughter of Sion, and shout aloud, O daughter of Jerusalem! Look, your king comes to you; triumphant and victorious is he, riding on an ass, on a colt, the foal of an ass. Then, listen: He will take from Ephraim the chariot, and from Jerusalem the horses of war. The bow of war will be broken. He will announce peace to the nations. His empire

will spread from sea to sea and from the river to the extremities of the earth. (Zechariah 9:9–10)

This is clearly a prophecy about Jesus. It tells that it is Jesus who will bring Peace—he is the Prince of Peace.

Jesus: Prince of Peace

Then some Greeks arrive and ask Philip if they can see Jesus. Philip speaks to Andrew, who approaches Jesus and says that some Greeks would like to see him. In the Gospel of John, the words for "want to see" signify "want to believe," that is, to see with the vision of faith. It is at this moment that Jesus, in a solemn manner, says: "The hour has come for the Son of Man to be glorified." The hour has come, the hour of his rejection and crucifixion. But the text reveals more. With the presence Greeks wanting to believe, it becomes clear that Jesus has come not only to liberate the Jews but to liberate all people, and to bring all people together. Jesus has come to break down the barriers and walls that separate people, so that they can meet each other and come together in oneness. Here we touch the heart of the revelation of Jesus and of his message; it is the promise of God made through the prophet Ezekiel to turn our hearts of stone into hearts of flesh. What does this promise mean? Jesus clearly told us, as we find in both Matthew and Luke: "I say to you: Love your enemies! Do good to those who hate you! Speak well of those who speak badly of you, and pray for those who persecute you!" (Luke 6:27). It is easy to love those who love us. Even sinners do that; anyone can do that. Here we are touching on the demands of love, the demands of this new love that Jesus wants to give to our world.

It is to open our hearts to all human beings.

St. Paul, who was profoundly Jewish and who was called to announce the Word of God, the word of Jesus, in Greece, said, "Jesus is our peace; he has made two peoples one, destroying in his flesh the walls that separate them" (Ephesians 2:14). Jesus has come to transform the deepest parts of our hearts and beings. He has come to bring us out from behind the walls of our culture, country, and class that give us security and part of our identity and lead us into a new love for all in the vast family of human beings. Jesus will give us a new gift: leading us and humanity into a deeper identity and to universal peace. This is the mission and the message of Jesus.

Alas, often we fail to understand that we are called to love the one that we fear, reject, or detest. At L'Arche we see this fear quite often; many people are afraid of those with a disability. They see them as a nuisance, as people who disturb their lives; they want to get rid of them or hide them away.

It seems that there is something that makes it impossible for us to love some people. We so quickly see what is negative in the other; their character, personality, or opinions annoy us. So very quickly, we judge them. Their culture is different from ours, so we judge it and see it as inferior. There is something in us that leads us to put down others, and to show we are better than them.

A Spirituality of Loss

Jesus, after saying that his hour has come, reveals a path to peace that at first glance seems painful and a source of anguish. There are three elements to this path. The first is loss, as Jesus says: "If a grain of wheat that falls to the ground does not die, it remains alone. However, if it dies, it bears much fruit" (John 12:14). These words are very strong! Jesus is surely speaking about his own death.

The mystery of Jesus is a mystery of weakness. From his wounded heart will flow blood and water. He will give life. There at the cross he will give us the Spirit of God, the Holy Spirit. But he has to die. This text does not only refer to Jesus, but it speaks also to each of us, teaching us that to the extent that we wish to protect our ego, our power, and our sense of being greater than others, we will remain alone. To give life, to work for unity and peace, there are things within us that must die. If we accept this death, then there is something even deeper within each of us, like what is hidden in the little grain of wheat, that will open as a powerful source of love and fruitfulness. When a grain of wheat falls into fertile soil, life will spring forth from it—perhaps forty, perhaps a hundred, other grains of wheat.

So this is the deepest understanding of what it means to be human. To become peacemakers, to give life, we must become familiar with the spirituality of loss, which implies anguish. There are things that we must lose, things that must die in us.

Dying to Our Egos

Jesus reveals the second element of the path: unity. He says: "If someone loves his own soul, he will lose it. If he separates himself from it in this world, he will have eternal life" (John 12:25).

What is this soul? Yes, there is the soul and the body. But here Jesus seems to be trying to point at our psychological compulsions. We have already spoken about the fear that is at the heart of every human being: the fear of not being recognized, of being cast aside, or of not having one's place. The fear of being rejected is something very deep within us. When confronted with fear and anguish, there are psychological forces that push us to want to win, to want to have the last word, to want to prove that we are important. How can we accept the anguish of loss?

Perhaps the biggest fear of human beings is to be abandoned by our friends, to be humiliated, to be a failure. Jesus is telling us that if we do not let ourselves be governed by this tremendous need to have the best place, if we accept not being the winner, and if we accept the anguish of loss, then we will have eternal life; Even in this world, we will have life, the life of God.

There was a young man who wanted to win in the Special Olympics, the Olympic Games for people with disabilities. He prepared himself, determined to win the gold medal. The moment of the final race arrived. He ran all out, longing to win. On the next lane ran another who also hoped to win the gold medal, and who suddenly tripped and fell. The first young man, seeing his neighbor fall, stopped running, offered his competitor his hand, and helped him up. The two runners came in last, hand in hand. The first man had accepted to lose the medal but to win unity and love.

This is a wonderful example of how it sometimes happens that people who are the most vulnerable have a lot to teach the so-called normal people. All too often, at the mercy of our egoistic compulsions, we wish to win at any cost. We want to prove that we are the best.

To Serve the Broken

There is a third element of the path toward peace that Jesus reveals, namely, knowing we are loved by God: "If someone would serve me, he will be with me. Where I am, there my servant will be also, and my Father will honor him" (John 12:26). If we serve Jesus in the poor, his Father will honor us. When we do not seek our own honor and success, God is with us.

Ghadir is a young woman who was welcomed into our L'Arche community in Bethany, in the Holy Land. She is a Muslim with cerebral palsy. Each time that I visited, she was so beautiful, laughing—laughing with her whole body! She welcomed me each time, her whole body quivering with joy. Each time that I met her, I was deeply touched. There was a beauty in her, and I felt in communion with her. She awoke a deep tenderness within me, as would a small child. When a child looks at us in the eyes and smiles, something happens in our hearts. There is a welling up of life, love, and tenderness within us. Ghadir was for me a little prophet of peace. When I visited her family, I saw that people were brought together by this little girl, so weak and vulnerable. I even dare say that in her smile there was a glimmer of the look and the presence of God. She touched me deeply.

There was an eleven-year-old boy with a disability who was having his First Communion at a church in Paris. The Mass was very beautiful. After the service, there was a family cele-bration. The uncle, who was also the boy's godfather, went to the mother and said, "What a beautiful liturgy! Isn't it sad that the child did not understand any of it?" The mother was hurt by this remark, and tears came to her eyes. The child seeing her tears said to his mother: "Don't worry, mummy! Jesus loves me as I am!" He implied, "I don't need to be what my uncle would have wanted. I have the right to be myself. I do not need to win things. I don't have to be strong or great, only to be myself, because I am loved, just as I am."

This then is the treasure that Jesus wants to reveal, our deepest identity, that of the beloved. Being loved by God liberates us from our need to win, so that we can become artisans of peace in our world.

Jesus Calls Us to Be Disarmed

What is it that will make us desire peace? What will make us accept dying to our egoism and giving our lives? What will make us accept a spirituality of loss, so that there is no more war? Certainly, this is something we have to ask ourselves. What will make us become passionate for peace, thirsty for peace?

How is it that Sophie Scholl, a young woman of twenty-two years, chose to resist in the face of the Gestapo, by giving out tracts that explained how to resist a dictator? She had seen the horrors of war. She and her brother Hans had heard about what the SS was doing in Poland against the Jews. She was changed in her depths. Thus, some people discover universal brotherhood and sisterhood in the midst of the horrors of a cruel dictatorship.

Here is a story of what happened in Burundi in April 1997. In both Burundi and Rwanda, there were huge tensions between the Hutus and the Tutsis; these tensions led to the genocide in Rwanda. There was a school in Burundi where there were both Hutu and Tutsi youth studying together, under a wonderful priest who was helping them learn to love each other. They spoke together of their difficulty in sharing, given the familial and cultural traditions that made them suspicious of each other's tribe. They became bonded to each other. One day, a group of extremists came into the school and said, "Hutus this side, Tutsis over there." What the young people did was astonishing. They stayed hand in hand and said, "No, we are staying together. We will not separate." Forty of them were killed. They discovered the horror of prejudice, the horror of hate, the horror of extremism. They did not resist with force—they probably could not have even done so. Instead, they accepted their deaths. Brotherhood and sisterhood is stronger than death.

How may I welcome others, different and just as they are? How can I discover that, even though some may be different than me, in the depths of our beings we are the same and that we are all beautiful? I should not right away see the negative in others. All human beings are loved by God. Let us first see the good in the others, and not fix ourselves on the negative. On the other hand, when we look inside ourselves, let us see the negative in us, even the seeds of hatred that enable us to put others down.

If we try to see what is good in others and to accept what is broken in ourselves, we will come closer together, accepting one another as human beings created and loved by God. This spiritual growth is a double movement: growth in wonderment and growth in humility.

Here is a small text written by Athenagoras, who was the patriarch of Constantinople: "We must fight the most difficult war, which is the war against ourselves. We must disarm ourselves.... I have waged this war for many years, and it was terrible. Now, I am disarmed. I no longer fear anything, because love banishes fear. I am disarmed of the desire to be right, and of justifying myself by putting others down."[4]

I must be disarmed. This comes through a mysterious change of my heart. Jesus came to do this. He is our peace. He made two peoples into one people, destroying in his flesh the barriers that separated them. Jesus came to unite us all together in oneness. For that, he humbled himself and accepted anguish.

Having given these three elements to peace, Jesus continues: "Now my soul is in anguish. What shall I say: Father save me from this hour? But it is the very reason I have come to this hour" (John 12:27) Jesus bars his own anguish and continues to walk to the place of rejection.

He is calling us also to bar our anguish and to continue on the road. He meets us in the darkest parts of our humanity and yet calls us to continue on the road to light. "The light is with you for a little longer. Go on your way while you have the light, lest the darkness overtake you. While you have the light, believe in the light, that you may become children of the light" (John 12:35–36). Even if we must pass through darkness and anguish, let us become peacemakers in and with Jesus.

CHAPTER ELEVEN

Jesus Lowers Himself to Wash Our Feet
(JOHN 13:1–38)

Jesus had been in Bethany with Martha and Mary and Lazarus whom he loved. From Bethany, he went to Jerusalem, where he was acclaimed. At one moment, there was a meeting with several Greeks. It is then that Jesus realizes that his hour has come. His soul is anguished: "Father, save me from this hour." But he also says: "It is for this that I have come…. Father, glorify thy name!"

A few days later, Jesus is with his disciples at a special and sacred meal. We read in John 13: "Before the Feast of the Passover, Jesus, knowing that his hour had come, and having loved his own, loved them to the end, to the extreme."

The Work of a Slave
In the course of this meal, Jesus rises up and removes his outer robe, the robe that confers dignity. He puts a towel around his waist, takes a basin, puts water in it, and then kneels before his disciples and begins to wash the disciples' feet. This is a sign of his extreme love for them. He washes them with love.

Peter reacts: "Lord, *you* wash *my* feet?"

Jesus responds, "You do not understand now; later you will understand."

"No, you will *nev*er wash my feet!" Peter argues.

We can understand Peter. He has followed a strong and powerful Jesus. Until now, Jesus has been a leader of men—he is strong, he performs miracles, he speaks with authority, he is the Good Shepherd standing upright. The disciples are there to follow him. And now he kneels before them! For Peter this is a degrading gesture, a gesture of weakness; it is impossible! We can understand: If Jesus visited or appeared to us where we live, and started to wash the floor, we would be shocked. But Jesus answers Peter: "If I do not wash your feet, you can have nothing more to do with me. There would be no more sharing between us; you would no longer be my disciple, or my friend. In short, if I don't wash your feet, you can leave."

Peter, shaken, says: "Then not only my feet, but my head and my hands as well!" Peter does not understand. Do we understand?

This is a moment of crisis for the twelve, somewhat similar to the one they lived when Jesus offered his flesh to be eaten. Jesus is revealing that he wants to live a real friendship with them, a relationship not just of superiority, but of love.

The Pyramid Model

Peter has an understanding of society as a pyramid: at the top there is power, riches, privileges, and hopefully wisdom. At the bottom are slaves, people who have no function, people with disabilities, and immigrants. However, Jesus has another vision of the community that he will build: He will build a *body*. In this body, each person has a place—even the weakest parts. Even the most vulnerable and fragile members are important, and each one is called to become a friend of Jesus.

Paul said that in the body there are many parts, and the most fragile parts are indispensable to the whole, which is the Church (1 Corinthians 12:22–25). Furthermore, the least presentable parts are to be honored.

Peter cannot accept the vision of Jesus seemingly degrading himself. The terms that Jesus uses: "If I do not wash your feet, you will have no part with me," are severe, as if to say: "If I don't wash your feet, you can leave!"

These words of Jesus reveal something important. Jesus, kneeling as a slave, reveals to us the mystery of the Word made flesh. To kneel is not just a gesture of humility; it is the revelation of who God is, who Jesus is. He came as a servant to liberate us and to live a relationship of love with us. Paul says that Jesus, "who, though he was in the form of God, did not count equality with God a thing to be grasped, emptied himself and became as a slave" (Philippians 2:6–7).

The whole mystery of the Word incarnate, that God so loved the world that he sent his only Son to save us, to liberate us, is revealed here—in Jesus as a servant.

The Revelation of the Love of Jesus

Jesus washes the feet of his disciples—even the feet of Judas. He washes them with tenderness, even with joy. This gesture is one of communion and love through the body. He must have taken each foot with gentleness. As he *washes*, he cleanses their wounds with tenderness and compassion. He is saying to each one: "I have confidence in you, and I love you. Now, stand up. Stand up because I need you on your feet to go around the world to announce the Good News. You are here to *continue* my mission. I will give you the Holy Spirit so that you may rise up." Thus, the tenderness of Jesus is given to us so that we may arise to accomplish our mission. The washing is to cleanse us; it is a sign of communion and of love with us, and it transmits a new spirit to us, a spirit of humility so that each of us may become a presence of Jesus for others.

Do unto Others as I Have Done unto You

Jesus puts his robe back on, sits down, and says to them: "Do you understand what I have just done to you? You call me Master and Lord, and so I am, and if I the Lord and Master has washed your feet, so you must also wash each other's feet. This is the example that I have given you, so that you will do among yourselves what I have done for you. Truly, truly, the servant is not more important than the master. If you do this, you will be blessed."

This is very strong! He has never before issued such a strong command. He insists three times: "You must do what I have done to you. You must be servant leaders, humble and loving." In other words, Jesus is saying to us: "Yes I will raise you up, each of you, with your gifts, and you must grow with your gifts in the Holy Spirit and in your human qualities. But afterward, you must each kneel down; your role is to be the servant of others, to love them, and to raise them up."

The Difficulty in the Exercise of Power

The great danger for all of us as human beings—including those in the Church—is to love power. Power can turn us quickly upon ourselves and strengthen our egos. For us to become humble servants who are called to raise up our brothers and sisters is a difficult task.

We need to be given the Holy Spirit, who alone can change our hearts of stone into hearts of flesh, so that we don't seek our own importance, our own power, or our own need to be seen as admirable, as being the best of God's creation or the best of his Church. No, we are to raise up our brothers and sisters, so that each one can stand up and fulfill their gifts and mission.

St. Paul understood this very clearly when he said to the Philippians: "Complete my joy in having for each other the same love, the same spirit, and in humility considering others as superior" (Philippians 2:2–5). This is the vision of Jesus, a vision of love one for another.

Love at the Heart of L'Arche

At L'Arche we discovered quite early the importance of the washing of the feet. It is especially important for us because the people we serve are living with a disability of some sort, and may not always understand the Word of God or a text. So the gesture accompanying a text takes on a new importance.

In washing each other's feet on the Thursday before Easter, we have discovered that it is a moment of grace, an important moment, something that reveals the presence of Jesus and of the Holy Spirit. We are there to serve each other, to create a body together. The great longing of Jesus is for unity, the unity of all Christians, and the unity of all of the human family. To wash each other's feet is to fulfill in one way the prayer of Jesus "that they may be one."

During a meeting in Northern Ireland, I spoke to the leaders of various churches about Jesus washing the feet of his disciples. The Irish cardinal, some Catholic bishops, and the primate, as well as several bishops of the Church of Ireland and the Moderators of the Presbyterians and the Methodists, were present. After I had spoken of this gesture of Jesus, we washed each other's feet in little groups and prayed over one another.

Cardinal Sean Baptist Brady of Ireland spoke in the synod in Rome a few months later about that washing of the feet. He said it was a gesture of intercommunion between people of different churches and from different ecclesiastical communities. Although we cannot always participate together in the Eucharist, and eat the Body of Jesus together, we can at least wash each other's feet, in a moment of grace and unity. What Jesus wants is to bring together in unity all the dispersed children of God.

I lived another such experience, at the World Council of Churches in Geneva, where there were gathered 230 delegates from many different churches. There again we spoke together of the importance of the washing of the feet, and then we washed each other's feet. To see an Orthodox bishop wash the feet of an American Baptist woman pastor was very moving. It is such gestures that progressively will lead us toward unity.

The Betrayal

After Jesus has washed the feet of his disciples, there is a moment of extreme sadness and bewilderment. Perhaps he proclaims it with confidence, or perhaps it is a cry of anguish: "Truly, truly, one of you is going to betray me." Simon Peter was on one side of Jesus, and John, the beloved disciple, was on the other side. Peter says to John: "Psst! Ask him who it is." John, who is at that moment lying on the heart of Jesus, across his chest, asks: "Lord, who is it?" Jesus indicates, by a gesture of friendship, that it is Judas. Satan enters into Judas. He leaves. It is night.

It is at that moment that Jesus reveals his commandment, the new commandment, which is the essential focus of his message. The disciples are understandably upset by Jesus going down on his knees, and then again by his announcement that he will soon be leaving them. He now gives them his last will or testament: "My commandment is that you love one another as I have loved you. They will know that you are my disciples by the love you have for one another." Clearly, in the context of the washing of the feet, Jesus is saying, "They will know you are my disciples by the attitudes of humble service, communion, and forgiveness that you have one for another." On the other hand, all that comes from a desire to prove that we are better than others destroys love, and destroys the message of Jesus.

Let's reflect on the three disciples of Jesus who are the main actors in this chapter: Peter, John, and Judas.

Who is Peter, who reacts? In the Gospel of Matthew we read that Peter, at the moment Jesus reveals that "the Son of Man will suffer a lot at the hands of the high priests and the scribes and will be put to death," takes Jesus aside and says, "Please, God, no! That will never happen to you!" (Matthew 16:21–23).

Peter sees suffering as something evil. He cannot imagine that the Messiah will suffer; on the contrary, he must be a victorious Messiah, a king. The response of Jesus to Peter is strong: "Get behind me, Satan." He says that to Peter, whom he has just confirmed as "the Rock"! "Behind me, Satan! You are an obstacle, your words are human words and not divine." Here in the Gospel of John, Jesus says to Peter: "If I don't wash you, you can have no part with me; it's over." We sense that Peter is a good and loyal man, and he wants to follow Jesus, but he cannot tolerate weakness or suffering, especially not a weak Messiah, or a suffering Messiah. Peter is very human; he cannot understand that Jesus can save us through weakness.

We can find something similar today. There are many people who cannot understand that people living with a disability, in all their weakness, could be chosen by God. They cannot tolerate the idea that God is present in their extreme vulnerability. They think Jesus should abolish suffering, or at least they feel that children with disabilities should be hidden and put aside.

There is a mental block in Peter. To him, the Messiah must be a strong person, a winner. Of course, after Peter receives the Holy Spirit, his all-too-human words will disappear and become divine. He will understand Jesus weak and humble of heart.

John, on the other hand, the beloved disciple who was resting on the heart of Jesus, has complete trust in Jesus. John has undergone a radical change. At one moment, even Jesus called him a "son of thunder," and he was even probably part of the group who discussed who was the most important. Then something happened to John. When? Was it when Jesus washed his feet with such love? We do not know. In any case, now he is totally abandoned to Jesus; he knows that is loved by him. In John, there is a radical trust in Jesus. The beloved disciple reveals that we are all called to become beloved.

Who is Judas? It is said of Judas, even in chapter 6, that the devil was in him. In the three places where Judas is spoken of, it is as if he is angry at love. He loses faith in Jesus when Jesus speaks of dwelling in us if we eat his flesh. In Bethany, he is angry about the relationship of Mary with Jesus, and now he is angry as Jesus washes his feet. It is as if Judas cannot tolerate love. With Peter, it is a blockage that is a misunderstanding of who Jesus is, but that will change with the gift of the Holy Spirit. Peter is very human. With Judas, there is something deeper: He cannot tolerate love. Is Judas a man who has suffered a lot in his childhood? We do not know. We know that he killed himself, but we do not know what happened in the last moments before his death. Did Judas remember how Jesus looked as he washed Judas's feet and manifested his love to him? Maybe then Judas wept.

We are all called in some ways to be like John. All kinds of people are like Peter; they do not understand Jesus, but through the gift of the Holy Spirit, all can know and love Jesus. Perhaps there are men like Judas who cannot tolerate love and tenderness. We cannot judge them, but we can pray for them. We are all called to become one in the glory of the Father.

CHAPTER TWELVE

Jesus Promises the Paraclete

(JOHN 14–17)

After Jesus washed the feet of his disciples and insisted that they must wash one another's feet, Jesus announces with great sadness, "One of you will betray me." He reveals that it is Judas. Judas leaves. It is at this moment that Jesus, with great tenderness, says: "Little children, I will only be with you for a short time now." Jesus announces his departure and gives them his testament, his new commandment: "You must love one another as I have loved you. They will know you are my disciples by the love you have for one another" (see John 13).

Now, Jesus reveals how the Church will continue without his physical presence: He will leave. The disciples will stay. Others will come after them to continue to announce his message of liberation and peace.

The Work of Jesus

One cannot read chapters 14, 15, and 16 of John without seeing the incredible tenderness of Jesus. He says: "Do not let your hearts be anguished! You trust God; trust me!" Then he says: "In the home of my Father there are many dwelling places. I go to prepare a place for you. When I return, I will bring you close to me so that where I am you may be also." Oh, what a gentle Jesus! He is saying: "I am leaving you, but I will not leave you. I will always be with you. I will keep you close to me." In these words there is a sense of covenant and of tenderness. Thomas reacts and asks: "How will we know the way? Where are we going?" But Jesus declares: "I am the Way, the Truth, and the Life." There can be only one way, and that is with him. We cannot go to the Father except through Jesus. That is clear because he and the Father are one.

Then Philip interrupts and says, "Show us the Father, and that will satisfy us!" And Jesus responds: "You have been with me all this time, Philip, and still you do not know me. He who has seen me has seen the Father. I am in the Father, and the Father is in me."

We will soon discover that this disciple of Jesus is called to become one with Jesus, and follow in his footsteps toward martyrdom.

You Will Do the Works of Jesus

Jesus continues: "If you believe in me, you will do the works that I do, and even greater works." Can you imagine what the disciples are thinking? First of all, Jesus knelt down to wash their feet like a slave. Then, Jesus told them that he would soon be leaving. Now, he tells them that they will do the works he has done! They cannot understand. What are the works of Jesus that the disciples—and all of us—are called to do? Some may say the works of Jesus are his miracles, such as the resurrection of Lazarus, or the healing of the blind man. But no—the work of Jesus is to reveal the Father. Jesus reveals *who God is*—a God of goodness, compassion, and forgiveness. The work of Jesus is also to give life. And life is relationship. Thus, the work of the disciples is to lead people into a relationship with God through Jesus and to transmit life through the gift of the Holy Spirit. And Jesus adds: "Whatever you ask in my name, I will do it." Let us ask Jesus that we may do his work.

The Father Will Give You Another Paraclete

The disciples cannot understand—but the key to the question is to come. Jesus tells them: "If you love me, you will keep my commandments. I will ask the Father, and he will give you another Paraclete, to be with you forever. This is the spirit of truth that the world cannot receive, because it has not seen him. But you know him because he abides with you."

We have here the fulfillment of the promises given us by God through the prophets of the Old Testament. God promised through the prophet Ezekiel that he would "change the heart of stone into a heart of flesh. I will put my spirit in you" (Ezekiel 36:26–27). Through Joel he said: "I will spread my Spirit on all flesh" (Joel 3:1). And through Jeremiah, he promised: "I will put my law within them. And I will write it upon their hearts. I will be their God…for they shall all know me, from the least of them to the greatest" (Jeremiah 31:33). The Old Testament is a revelation of these new things that were to come.

We are now truly in Messianic times: the new covenant of love is being announced. The Spirit of God will be given to all, and he will give an entirely new vision of the world that will change the history of humanity. Jesus and the Father will put the Holy Spirit into the hearts of us all. As Jesus had said to Nicodemus: "To enter the kingdom of God one must be born of water and the Spirit," Jesus also says: "Do not be astonished that I say that you must be born from on high. The wind blows where it wills, and you hear the sound of it, but you do not know from where it comes, or where it goes. It is the same thing for those who are born in the Spirit." Something new will be given, so that we may be inspired and led by the Spirit. We will not always know where the Spirit will lead us. The important thing is to die to our ego and trust God.

Spirit and Paraclete

But who is this Paraclete Jesus speaks of? In the Old Testament there is no word like this one. The Greek word, *parakletos*, is made up of two Greek words, *para* and *kaleo*, which together mean "to call toward." So, *parakletos* is *"the one who answers a cry."* This is the new name of God. In the different translations of the Bible, parakletos is translated as *"defender," "advocate," "consoler,"* "intercessor," and so on. These words reflect the need of a weak person for someone strong to help them or speak on their behalf. Thus, the Paraclete is the one who speaks in the name of, defends, protects, and consoles the weak person. This new name of God is different than another name: *Spiritus. Spiritus*, or Spirit, is translated as *"wind,"* or *"breath."* It is the Spirit that inspires. The Spirit was given to the prophets; it is a movement, an enthusiasm, life given. It is strong and beautiful. Para*k*let*o*s and Spiritus are one and the same, the third person of the Trinity.

Parakletos is the Spirit caring for a weak person. A mother looking after her baby is a parakletos. She attends to the needs of her baby and watches over, protects, and consoles the baby. *Parakletos* is not merely an activity, something that is done, but it is a caring relationship. On the other hand, *Spiritus* is like a force that is given to us and incites us to move forward. When someone is weak and feels all alone and vulnerable, he or she does not necessarily need someone filled with energy, a *spiritus*, who can do things, but rather a *parakletos*, someone who says with tenderness: "I love you. I love you just as you are."

Parakletos is therefore an important name. It is the revelation of the *presence of God* when we are weak. It is the response of God to a cry, the cry of the child. The psalms tell us that God listens to the cry of the poor. The cry of the poor is not primarily for money, work, or things but for a relationship of respect, love, and trust. The *Parakletos* reveals to the individual: "You are important. You have value. I am with you so that you can rediscover your dignity."

This is also the reality of L'Arche. At L'Arche, we are not there just to take care of people with disabilities, or do things for them; we are there to live with them, so that each may discover this truth: "You are loved as you are. You have the right to be yourself. Our desire is to help you rise up so that you may develop your gifts and become fully yourself."

So, the Holy Spirit, the Paraclete, is given to reveal to us that we are loved by God and called by God. St. Paul will tell us that it is the Spirit that allows us to cry, "Abba! Father!" because the Holy Spirit reveals to us that we are truly children of God called to grow in love.

Jesus and the Father Will Come

Jesus, having revealed that he would send the Spirit of truth, tells his disciples: "If someone loves me, he will keep my word [logos], my Father will love him, and we will come to him and make in him our dwelling place."

Here we have something new! If we keep the word of Jesus, we will become the temple of God—*the* dwelling place of

God. For the Jewish people of ancient times, the Temple was truly the dwelling place of God. But now, it is each one of us who will be God's dwelling place. A disciple of Jesus is the new temple.

There is a beautiful prayer that Cardinal Newman wrote. This little prayer is also used by the sisters of Mother Teresa, who say it daily:

> Dear Jesus, help me to spread your fragrance wherever
> I go.
> Flood my soul with your spirit and life.
> Penetrate and possess my whole being so utterly that
> my life may only be a radiance of yours.
> Shine through me and be so in me
> That every soul I come in contact with
> May feel your presence in my soul.
> Let them look up and see no longer me, but only
> Jesus!
>
> Stay with me and then I will begin to shine as you
> shine,
> So to shine as to be a light to others;
> The light, O Jesus, will be all from you; none of it
> will be mine.
> It will be you, shining on others through me.
>
> Let me thus praise you in the way which you love
> best, by shining on those around me.
> Let me preach you without preaching, not by words
> but by example,
> By the catching force, the sympathetic influence of
> what I do,

the evident fullness of the love my heart bears to you. Amen.[5]

As Jesus said, "The Father and I are one." We, too, as his disciples are called to become one with Jesus and the Father. For this we must be purified and die to ourselves, continuing on the path where Jesus comes to dwell within us more and more. Then, when Jesus lives within us, he will also act through us.

Jesus as the True Vine

That is why Jesus says, "I am the vine. You are the branches. And to bear this fruit we must be pruned, so that we can bear even more fruit" (John 15:5).

Jesus says that it is to the glory of the Father that we bear much fruit. Is it I who bears the fruit, or is it Jesus who bears the fruit? It is Jesus in me, and me in Jesus; we are one in each other. Together we bear fruit and give life. We are called to give God's love, and so to give hope.

Jesus did not come into this world so that we would be productive, build beautiful buildings, make things, and so on. It is, of course, good to make things, but that is not the heart of the Gospel! The heart of the Gospel is relationship—it is to be liberated of our egos in order to love and give life.

Relationship is about communicating life to one another. The fecundity of relationship is when life, love, and hope pass between us. God is life and gives life. We, too, are called to give life. And in order to give life, we must be pruned.

The vine is pruned. The prunings are all those catastrophes that fall unexpected upon our lives, all the moments of loss and grief: loss of work, relationship, reputation, health—all those accidents that seem to take away life. We feel crushed, depressed, broken. We are like vines in winter: pruned back to a small stump of wood. These vines appear to be completely without life. But no! When spring arrives, tiny buds appear, and then the leaves, and then the grapes: There is life! Each of us lives those dark moments of loss that bring grief. It is never easy when the vine of our lives is cut back and life disappears. Jesus is telling us that there is pruning, yes, but it is in order that we might bear more fruit. We must pass through various crises to find the life of the Spirit.

The danger for us is to attach ourselves to forms of life that are not the life of Jesus and the Spirit. These forms of life can be very human, even quite wonderful, such as in the political or the social field, in our creative capacities, and in teaching. We can do very good work in all sorts of fields.

However, when we fall sick, or something appears broken in our lives, then we often rediscover our spiritual lives and what it means to be inspired by the Spirit. We discover then that living in the Spirit is not simply a matter of doing things for God, but rather entering into communion with God. If we let ourselves be drawn into communion with God, and drink the water promised by Jesus, we will live what he said to the Samaritan woman: "The water that I will give will become in the person who drinks it a spring of water welling up to eternal life!" We will receive the life of God. And if we receive the Spirit, we will transmit the Spirit.

Dwell in Jesus and Become His Friend

In this chapter Jesus is revealing the heart and the goal of the Gospel: that we might become his friends. "Dwell in my love, as I dwell in the love of my Father! These things I have said to you so that my joy may be with you and that your joy be full." The joy of Jesus will be in us, and our joy will be complete. Jesus wants us to become men and women of joy, fully happy, fully joyful. Why joyful? Not because we make or build things, but because we are with Jesus and dwell in him in order to give life. Then Jesus reveals, "I no longer call you my servants. I call you my friends. For all that I have heard from my Father I have made known to you." He adds, "It is I who have chosen you. You did not choose me." The heart of the Gospel of John is there. We have been chosen by God to become beloved of Jesus. What is required of us is to welcome and accept this choice and call, to accept that the Holy Spirit is given to us so that we may love each other as Jesus loves. There will be pruning moments of loss and inner pain, but this is so we will become progressively more like Jesus.

To become like Jesus does not mean that we always feel peaceful and loving. To become like Jesus also means to suffer as he did, to be rejected as he was. While Jesus was suffering and in pain, he was always in relationship with his Father. He never leaves this relationship of love. He is always with his Father, saying, "Not my will, but yours." All that he desires is the will of his Father. Although to become like Jesus can also mean for us to enter into anguish and agony as he did, we are called to do the will of Jesus and the will of the Father, and to trust that he is always there with us and in us.

Our Final Destiny

Finally we come to chapter 17 of John, which is a sort of summit of the Gospel. It is a prayer for the unity of humanity, unity for which we were made. The prologue of John is the descent of the Word into flesh, into the flesh of Mary. Chapter 17 is the return of Jesus to the Father with all his friends, with all humanity. It is with all men and women together that Jesus yearns to return to the Father. The great longing of the Father, one with Jesus, is to live in community with all men and women. "I pray, Father, that you in me, and I in you, and they in us, will all be perfectly one," prays Jesus. God longs that we will all be perfectly one in him and with him for his glory and the glory and joy of all creation.

CHAPTER THIRTEEN

Jesus Humiliated, Abandoned, Suffering, in Communion with Mary

(JOHN 18–19)

The hour of Jesus has come, the hour in which he will give his life—in which he will give *life*, in superabundance. After having washed the feet of his disciples, given them his new commandment, and promised to send them the Holy Spirit, the Paraclete, Jesus prays for his disciples: "Holy Father, keep them in your name that they may be one as we are one. May they have the plenitude of my joy. Keep them from the evil one. Sanctify them in the truth. I do not pray only for them, but also for all those who will believe through their word. I pray, Father, that you in me, and I in you, and they in us, will all be perfectly one. Father, may the love with which you have loved me dwell in them, and I in them."

Now, with his disciples, Jesus goes to the Garden of Olives, a place where they often met together to share and to pray. Judas knew it as well. It is here that he brings a troop of Roman soldiers and the temple guards. They arrest Jesus and take him, bound, to Annas and then on to Caiaphas. It is there near the court of the high priest that Peter denies Jesus.

Peter's Denial
One of the servants seeing Peter says: "You are one of his disciples."

"No, I am not." replies Peter. And a second time: "*No,* I am *not.*"

Matthew says that Peter, swearing and cursing, cries out: "I do not know this man!" (Matthew 26:72).

What is going on? One gets the impression that Peter is in a breakdown or a state of collapse. He had an idea of who Jesus is. He had an ideology of Jesus. He had followed a strong Jesus, the Messiah who would do great things, who had done miracles, and who spoke with authority. Jesus was strong, the victorious Messiah. Now he discovers that Jesus is weak: Jesus is not speaking; he is not defending himself. Peter sees now that Jesus will be condemned to death. Indeed, he does not know the weak Jesus; he knows only the strong Jesus. He is a disciple of the strong Jesus. Peter, in denying Jesus, lives a psychological breakdown, a collapse of his own identity.

Some people today are similarly upset when they see the weaknesses of the Church. They want a strong Church, a victorious Church, a Church that will do wonderful things. When they see the weakness of the Church, without sufficient priests, with the anguishing stories of pedophilia, they are upset. They turn from the Church: "I do not know this Church."

Jesus before Pilate

Jesus is led from Caiaphas and the Jewish authorities to Pilate. Let us consider these three protagonists.

Caiaphas and the Jewish authorities want to get rid of Jesus, whose presence is a danger for them. We read in John 11 that the high priest calls together the Sanhedrin, the Jewish authorities who are scared of Jesus, and says: "People are starting to believe in him. We have to get rid of him so that he does not start a revolt, which might provoke the Romans to retaliate, destroying our nation and our holy places" (John 11:45–50).

They are afraid. They are also angry at Jesus because they interpret Jesus as saying that he is God, that he is the Son of God. For them this sounds like blasphemy. However, Jesus had tenderly explained that the Father is greater than he, and that he can do nothing without the Father revealing it to him. Fundamentally, they want to get rid of Jesus because he opens the door to something radically new. He brings a new love. He calls people to have confidence in him, saying that people will then become liberated, liberated from fear and the slavery of sin. Above all, to accept this new message of Jesus, one must be reborn in love. Change is required; one must be transformed. There is something in the authorities that refuses change. They cling to the status quo, and to their power. They are frightened.

Then there is Jesus. He is serene; he says little, and sometimes he is silent. Jesus is serene because he is led by love and by his unity with his Father. Jesus is different at the hour of his suffering. It is as if he is carried by love and drawn to give life. His suffering is for life. When someone is carried by love, he moves gently and serenely toward suffering, knowing that it leads to liberation and to the gift of the Spirit. Jesus came to witness to the truth; he is engulfed in peace.

There is also Pilate. Pilate is a weak man, who hates and scorns the Jews. Like many weak people, he is capable of great violence. Jesus is led before Pilate by the Jewish authorities, with the hope that Pilate will condemn Jesus. It is before

Pilate that Jesus affirms that he is king. In John 6 the people had wanted to make Jesus king, but he slipped away. He did not want to be an earthly or temporal king. Jesus is now before Pilate, a king in chains. He is the king of our hearts, the king of love. Perhaps it is Jesus in chains who draws people, helping them to discover that all those who are in chains, imprisoned, and tortured carry within them a mysterious presence of God, a mysterious dignity, a sacredness.

Pilate has Jesus flogged, scourged, and crowned with thorns. The Roman soldiers make fun of Jesus, mock him, humiliate him. They put a crown on his head, a crown of thorns. They put a purple robe around him. "Hail, King of the Jews!" They laugh at him. The body of Jesus is by now extremely vulnerable, weak, fragile, and sensitive. Here is the Lamb of God, the body of Jesus, totally vulnerable, yet beautiful and exquisitely sensitive. This silent, gentle vulnerability of Jesus perhaps evokes a sort of sadism in the soldiers, who hit him and spit on him, shouting and laughing, "Hail, King of the Jews!"

Pilate, however, finds no reason to condemn Jesus. He says: "Should I condemn your king?" The chief priests answer, "We have no king other than Caesar!"—the ultimate blasphemy. Pilate is afraid that they will denounce him to the emperor and that he will lose his position of power. He agrees to condemn Jesus and hands him over to them to be crucified. Pilate is frightened.

Jesus: Victim and Savior

They lead Jesus outside the walls of Jerusalem, where they crucify him between two others. Jesus is in the middle of the three because Jesus is in the middle of history, opening the door to the kingdom of heaven.

John, with great solemnity, speaks of four events. The first is to affirm the universal kingship of Jesus. The inscription is over his head in three languages—Hebrew, Greek, and Latin: "Jesus of Nazareth, King of the Jews." Jesus is the king, a crucified king. The chief priests want Pilate to write, "He *says* he is king of the Jews," but Pilate refuses, saying, "What is written, is written." It was a way for Pilate to further humiliate both Jesus and those Jews who wanted him dead.

Jesus then is stripped of his clothes; he is stripped of his exterior robe and of his tunic, which was made entirely from one piece of cloth. He is naked. Here we have the answer, though perhaps not in its entirety, to what Adam said. God had said to him, "Adam, where are you?" And Adam had replied, "I was frightened because I was naked, and so I hid." Jesus is naked, but in his nakedness he exposes who he is: "I AM." He is God. For us human beings, our nakedness reveals that we are not God. Our bodies are finite. We did not exist several years ago, and we will not exist in a few years. We hide our poverty in clothing.

Jesus is stripped naked; he is exposed. Isaiah describes the suffering and rejected servant, whom we, as Christians, understand as prophetically revealing Jesus:

> Like a sapling he grew up before us, without beauty, comeliness, or charm, despised, a man of sorrows acquainted with grief. He was scorned and cast aside. It was by his wounds that we were healed. (Isaiah 53:2–5)

Jesus is humiliated, abandoned, excluded. When he has been crucified, Matthew's Gospel tells us the high priests and scribes shout: "You have saved others, now save yourself!" and they laugh at him. Jesus has been abandoned by his friends. This was only a few days after the people had been acclaiming him with shouts of "Hosanna, Hosanna, Son of David!" On the day of his crucifixion, the chief priests cry out, "Crucify him! Crucify him!" He has disappointed them. Jesus is humiliated and excluded by the leaders of his own people—as well as, of course, the Roman occupiers, who alone had the power to crucify him.

Let us think of the terrible pain of Jesus, a Jew, excluded by the Jewish people. His deepest identity is as a Jew. He is Jewish in his whole being; his human heart was formed in the beautiful Jewish tradition. Jesus the Jew is condemned and cast off by the leaders of his own people. It is as if he has lost his deepest identity. He lives a radical and utter failure, rejection, and mockery. Jesus is completely vulnerable because of this, in addition to his atrocious physical suffering— his naked body covered in blood from the flogging, done by cords embedded with tiny metal pieces that tear the skin. Jesus is before us, humiliated, naked, and bleeding.

Mary: Woman of Compassion

At the cross, Mary is standing close to him. What is Mary living? We know that Peter fled. Peter could not tolerate Jesus fragile, humble, little, silent, and downtrodden. He said, "No, I do not know this man." How is it that Mary is there, standing as close as possible to him?

Mary has always known the weakness of Jesus. She had held the tiny Jesus in her arms, she had fed him her milk, she had loved him, she had touched him with tenderness, and she had looked after him when he was little. When he cried, she was there to console him and to love him. Mary does not fear a humble, little, and vulnerable Messiah. What is Mary's experience as she stands near him at the cross?

Mary does not seem to be weeping because she has lost a son. The whole attitude of Mary is to be there beside her beloved son, humiliated, excluded, a failure, and suffering. She is there with all her being, all her love, to sustain him and to help him and be with him. Jesus is in a radical and total state of vulnerability, and Mary says, "I am with you. I trust you." It is as if Mary represents all of humanity in front of Jesus, who came to love and save all of humanity. Her presence says: "I am with you and I love you."

Mary is standing. She is a woman who sustains, consoles, and strengthens, in some way saying, "I offer myself to the Father with you, in you, and for you, for the salvation of the world." Mary knows that Jesus's hour has come. The hour of the liberation of humanity from the forces of evil has come, the moment when the prince of this world will be cast aside.

Mary is a woman of compassion. There are two kinds of compassion. First, there is compassion-competence. When there is suffering, it is necessary to alleviate it; when someone is hungry, it is important that food be provided. Similarly, when there are issues that can be resolved on the political, social, or medical domains, people much act in truth and in justice. We need to do everything we can on a practical level, a level of competence, to ensure that people do not become engulfed needlessly in a world of suffering. We must help them to rise up.

There is also compassion-presence. When a mother loses a child, there is nothing we can do. When a mother discovers her child has a severe disability and she is grieving, there is nothing to do but be with her. "To be with," is the compassion of presence. It says: "You are not alone; I am with you. This suffering is not a punishment or an infliction. I am with you, in you, to help you rise up."

John, the beloved disciple, is also there with Mary at the foot of the cross. Jesus says to him: "Woman, here is your son; John, here is your mother." Jesus does not say, "Look after *my* mother." He says, "Here is *your* mother." After that moment, John took her as his own mother. Sometimes the passage is translated as saying he "took her home," but that does not reflect what is most important here. The text actually says, "He took her as his own." Perhaps it might even be read more strongly as, "He took her as his treasure."

Jesus then cries out, "I am thirsty." Finally, he declares, "All is accomplished." Jesus inclines his head and gives up his Spirit. His mission is complete. His last words of accomplishment had been to ask Mary to love John and guide him as a mother, as she had mothered Jesus.

The high priests want to ask Pilate to remove the bodies of the three crucified men before the Feast of the Passover. So, the soldiers come to kill him, but Jesus is already dead. One of the soldiers pierces the side of Jesus with a spear, and blood and water flow forth. When John speaks of this, he does so forcefully, insisting, "I was a witness. I saw it, and my testimony is true." He saw blood and water and flowing from the heart of Jesus. We know that throughout the Gospel John has revealed that water is the symbol of the Spirit. So, after Jesus said, "Everything is accomplished" and after water and blood came out of Jesus, John became conscious that everything would begin as Jesus promised: the gift of the Holy Spirit would be given at Pentecost. All is not finished; all is just beginning!

CHAPTER FOURTEEN

Jesus, Risen, Calls Each One by Name
(JOHN 20:11–23; 21)

The Gospel of John started with a marvelous relationship that is the source of all relationships: In the beginning was the Logos, and the Logos was in relationship with God, and the Logos was God. Now, it finishes with another beautiful relationship.

On this day, close to the tomb where the body of Jesus had been laid, we find Mary of Magdala, her heart filled with grief. She is a woman who has suffered a broken relationship. She was plunged into a kind of solitude, anguish, and depression because the one she loved is dead, under atrocious and traumatizing conditions. Her heart is profoundly broken! On this first day of the week, Mary of Magdala comes to the tomb because she wants to anoint the body of the one she has loved with aromatic oils.

The Encounter with Mary of Magdala
But when she arrives, she discovers that the huge stone that had covered the tomb has been moved. Jesus's body is not there! Someone has stolen the body of the one she loves! So, she runs to the disciples and tells them: "Someone has stolen the body of my Lord!" Peter and the beloved disciple come running, and they see that the tomb is empty. They depart, leaving Mary of Magdala alone and in tears.

She looks into the tomb one more time. She sees two angels, one at the head of the place where Jesus had lain, and the other at the foot. They ask her: "Why are you crying?" She is so blinded by her tears, her melancholy, and her grief that she does not ask herself what the two angels are doing there. If *we* saw two angels, we might stop and ask a few questions. But in her sorrow, she is unable to recognize the signs of God. She is blinded by her tears. When we are grieving, it is important to try to see the signs of God that call us to come out of our grief, and to live.

Finally, she turns around, and what does she see? She sees a man, whom she takes to be the gardener. This man is in fact Jesus, but she does not recognize him.

He says, "Woman, why are you crying? Who are you looking for?"

Mary replies, "If it is you who has taken the body of my Lord, tell me where you have put him, so that I may go and find him and take him away."

"Mary."

Jesus must have said Mary's name with a tone of exquisite tenderness, with the tone of a lover. Jesus is not just saying, "Hello!" No, he says her name, and he says it with tenderness. Jesus's face must have been shining with joy!

Mary is obviously thrilled to see Jesus alive, and Jesus is infinitely joyous to meet Mary of Magdala as well. Jesus is deeply thankful because she was there at the cross.

It is important to understand that a woman who had been taken up in the world of prostitution was present at the cross. Mary was from the town of Magdala, which was not far from

Jerusalem, in Galilee, and it was there that there was a Roman encampment. Of course, where there was a Roman encampment, there would be prostitution. The significance of insisting on associating her name with that place is that it indicates that she is a prostitute. At the cross were the women full of grace; the women forgiven and loved.

Mary is overcome with joy at the beautiful encounter: "It is true; it is he whom my heart loves! He is alive!" She throws herself at his feet. "Rabboni!" she cries. "Master! My love!" This is a most extraordinary moment in this relationship.

When we read, "Jesus called her by her name," we are taken back to the words of Isaiah 43: "Be not afraid. I have redeemed you. I have called you by your name, and you are mine." We are bounded together with God in a covenant of love:

> You are mine. If you pass though the rivers, I will always be with you. If you are in deep waters, you will not drown. If you pass through fire, you will not be burned. Because I am the God of Israel, your Savior; you are precious to my eyes, and I love you. Do not be afraid, for I am with you. (Isaiah 43:1–5)

So, when Jesus calls Mary by her name, he thus reveals the covenant: "I will always, always be with you!"

With Jesus there before her, Mary puts her arms around him, apparently thinking, "Now that I have him here, I won't let him leave. I want to be with you forever. You are my Beloved, and I love you." Mary at the foot of the cross and now at the feet of Jesus is the sign of a beautiful disciple of Jesus. This Gospel teaches us all to become a beloved friend of Jesus.

But Jesus says to her, "Do not hold on to me. I have not yet gone to the Father. Go to the brothers. Tell them I will go up to my Father and your Father, to my God and your God." Then he sends her off.

It must have been difficult for her to be sent off to the *brothers* who had not been very friendly to her and who were not at the cross!

We see, in both St. Mark and St. Luke, that when she goes to them, they do not believe her! They think that she is talking nonsense or hallucinating, as she tells them, "I saw him! I saw him! He lives!"

This conflict between men and women still exists today. The disciples may not have wanted Mary with her vibrant nature to be around. Jesus tells each of us as well: "Go! Go into your community. Go to the brothers" (see Mark 16:9–11 and Luke 24:9–11). There will be suffering, but community life is essential. If anyone wants to think of himself or herself as a saint, go and live alone! When we live in community, we discover very quickly that we are not. All kinds of things get stirred up. There are people we like a lot and whom we become attached to, and there are others whom we like less, because they stir up anguish in us. Community is a place that is both beautiful and painful; but it is also the place of transformation. Community offers us the opportunity to become men and women who make an effort to grow in love, an effort that will always be crowned by the power of the Holy Spirit, who teaches us to love as Jesus loved.

The Appearance to the Disciples

Evening comes and Jesus stands among his disciples in the upper room. They are inside, with the doors closed, and he comes into their midst. They are grieving and afraid of the Jewish authorities. Mary of Magdala is a woman grieving for her beloved, but she is ardent in love and not frightened; she was at the cross, unlike the disciples, except John.

"Peace to you," Jesus says, showing them his hands and his side. "It is really I. Peace to you." When Jesus said, "Peace," it was probably a little like when he looked at Mary and said her name. Each one there likely felt reunited with the presence of Jesus, who had told them, "I love you. I live a covenant with you. I will always be with you. You are precious in my eyes, and I love you." Jesus reminds the apostles that he lives a relationship with them that has transformed them.

The Commissioning

What is the mission of Jesus? It is to announce the Good News to the poor, the deliverance of captives, the restoration of sight to the blind, and the liberation of the oppressed. He came to save all those who are downtrodden and unable to live life fully.

Jesus now sends his disciples, not to say, "God loves you in Jesus," but to say, "I, a disciple of Jesus, love you, and I commit myself to work with you in the name of Jesus." That is the mission that Jesus gives to the Church—a mission of compassion and goodness. It is a mission to reveal to human beings their beauty, that each one is a child of God, and that in each one the beauty of God himself is found. Each of us—including those taken up in the world of drugs, or those crushed by suffering or bombs—is loved by God.

The vision of Jesus is for a renewal of the world—a vision in which all human beings begin to break down and overcome the walls separating us from one another, so that we may all become one. Jesus sends his disciples out to announce this Good News to the poor. But they know now that they cannot do it alone, that they do not have the strength. Just as their fear of the Jews locked them in a room, they have inner fears and inner barricades as well. They need the power of the Holy Spirit.

So, Jesus breathes on each one, saying, "Receive the Holy Spirit." There is something extraordinarily beautiful here. Jesus is telling each one, "You will not be able to do this all alone. If you think you can, there is the risk that you will become caught up in yourself and in thinking you are someone special." We are not someone special; our deepest identity is to be friends of Jesus. He sends us to enter into relationship with the poor and the oppressed. We, the disciples of Jesus, will discover that Jesus is hidden in the poor, and that it is he who will change us, through our relationship with them. That is why each of us needs this new force that will bring down our systems of protection, the walls that are created by fear. Jesus wants to liberate us from fear, in giving us a new force, which is the power of the Holy Spirit.

Then Jesus calls them to be signs of forgiveness. The unique role of the disciple of Jesus is to forgive. But forgiveness is not a grandiose act; it is to enter into relationship with the poor and to raise each one up, saying, "You are you, and you are important." It is clear that if others accepts this love, their sins are forgiven and we are in communion; there is a relationship. However, if they refuse this love, then the shadows persist in them. It is in the measure that we love others as they are—and that others accept to be loved by this love, which does not come from ourselves but from the Father—that the shadows are overcome. The whole message of Jesus is: "Be compassionate as your Father is compassionate. Do not judge, and you will not be judged. Do not condemn, and you will not be condemned. Forgive, and you will be forgiven." This forgiveness comes through relationship, because we love and welcome the love of one another.

All Seems So Ordinary

A few days later, the risen Jesus is standing on the shores of the Lake of Galilee. The disciples, under the guidance of Peter, had embarked the previous night in their little boat to go fishing. They had worked all night, without catching anything. Now, at dawn, they see a man standing on the shore. This man calls out:

"Hey, children, did you catch anything?"

"No," they call back.

"Cast the nets on the other side."

So the disciples cast their nets on the other side of the boat, and immediately the nets are filled with many fish.

The beloved disciple recognizes Jesus right away. He cries, "It is the Lord!" So Peter throws himself into the water, rushing to be with Jesus. Jesus has prepared a small fire on the beach, with some fish and some bread. Jesus says simply and with much tenderness, because he loves these men: "Come, have some breakfast."

What delicacy! It is a small gesture—he has prepared a fire. The fish is warm, and so is the bread. They eat their breakfast, happy to be with Jesus.

Then Jesus takes Peter aside. It is a serious moment, grave even.

"Simon, son of John: Do you love me more than these others?"

"You know everything, Lord. You know that I love you!"

"Feed my lambs."

Then Jesus asks again, "Simon, son of John: Do you love me?"

"You know everything, Lord. You know that I love you!"

"Tend my sheep."

And a third time, Jesus asks, "Simon, Son of John: Do you love me?"

"You know everything, Lord. You know that I love you!"

"Feed my sheep."

Peter had denied Jesus three times. Now, he says three times, "You know that I love you!" Not only is Peter forgiven; he is confirmed in his role as the Rock.

After that, Jesus says to Peter, "When you were young, you put on your own belt, and you went where you wanted. When you grow old, someone else will put on your belt and will lead you where you do not want to go. Follow me."

Then Peter turns around and sees the beloved disciple. He asks Jesus, "What about him, Lord?" Jesus has confirmed Peter as the shepherd of the flock. What will become of John who was at the foot of the cross with Mary? Jesus responds: "If I want him to dwell until I return, what does it matter to you? You, follow me!"

As we have seen, the word dwell is at the heart of the Gospel of John. It began with the two disciples asking Jesus, "Where do you dwell?" Jesus answered: "Come and see" (John 1:38, 39). This Gospel has led us "to dwell in Jesus," to become his beloved friends. The last word of Jesus in this Gospel is that the message of John will remain, or dwell, until the end of time when Jesus returns.

That is the end of the Gospel of John. The sun is rising, the sun of hope, because Jesus is clearly the Light of the world, and he is calling us all to become his beloved friends.

1. To discover more about L'Arche and Faith and Light, please visit www.larche.org and www.faithandlight.org.

2. Etty Hillesum, *An Interrupted Life: The Diaries of Etty Hillesum, 1941–43*, trans. Arnold Pomerans (New York: Pantheon, 1983), p. 151.

3. John Paul II, International Symposium on the Dignity and Rights of the Mentally Disabled Person, 6, January 4, 2004.

4. Quoted in Olivier Clément, *Dialogue avec le Patriarche Athenagoras* (Paris: Fayard, 1976), p. 180.

5. Quoted in Jean Maalouf, *Praying with Mother Teresa* (Frederick, Md.: Word Among Us, 2000), p. 108.